The Covid pandemic has challenged us all to reimagine the healthcare of the future. This book makes a compelling case to start in the community and in the home, and with patients themselves. Shantanu has a knack for seeing around the corner and being able to bridge where the system is today to where it needs to be. In this new book, he shares a powerful framework that healthcare leaders globally can use to accelerate progress on health for the world's most vulnerable.

—Mickey Chopra, MD, PhD, Global Solutions Lead for Service Delivery in the Health Nutrition and Population global practice of the World Bank and former Chief of Health at UNICEF

Dr. Nundy's book is a must-read for anybody who has tried to understand how we can take a catastrophe such as the pandemic and our lack of a national response and try and emerge as a stronger nation. His insights are practical yet sophisticated because he brings his clinical instincts, his business acumen, and his heart to each page. There will be a number of books that reflect on 2020 and beyond, but *Care After Covid* should be at the top everyone's reading list.

—Kavita Patel, MD, MSHS, NBC News contributor, MSNBC columnist, and Nonresident Fellow at the Brookings Institution

We're at the start of a new golden era for tech-enabled healthcare, and Shantanu Nundy artfully illustrates the primary forces that are driving the reimagination of our care delivery system from the ground up. Shantanu's work is a call to arms for both innovators who are building virtual-first care models, as well as incumbents who will need to reinvent themselves to stay relevant in the post-pandemic "next normal."

—Julie Yoo, General Partner at Andreessen Horowitz

Dr. Nundy represents the best of American medicine—a Johns Hopkins–trained physician and MIT engineer who has spent a career inventing new ways of delivering healthcare and caring for the underserved. In *Care After Covid*, Shantanu translates his experiences into a bold and compelling vision for where healthcare must go that will resonate with providers and C-suite leadership alike.

—SENATOR BILL FRIST, former US Senate Majority Leader and heart and lung transplant surgeon

Too many in healthcare are asking how we can "get back to normal," rather than how we can work to use this crisis to create a new, better normal for patients. Nundy asks the right questions to help envision the future we need.

—SACHIN H. JAIN, MD, MBA, President and CEO of SCAN Group and Health Plan and Adjunct Professor at Stanford University School of Medicine

Care After Covid is essential reading for anyone in healthcare who seeks to turn understanding into action. Writing with a sense of urgency and grounded in his clinical practice, Dr. Nundy helps us look around the corner at what could be in our post-pandemic reality. His imagination and vision are rooted in a humility that offers fresh perspectives on healthcare delivery.

—DAVE A. CHOKSHI, MD, MSc, New York City Health Commissioner

Nundy shares an ambitious but achievable vision of a healthcare system that works better for patients and their caregivers. Despite our visible failings throughout the pandemic, I share his view of a hopeful future and look forward to our growing coalition of those willing to bring it to life!

—ANEESH CHOPRA, President of CareJourney and former US Chief Technology Officer

Out of a public health crisis, a healthcare revolution has been born. Dr. Shantanu Nundy, a brilliant, visionary physician innovator, provides a road map to the future of health in the twenty-first century. This landmark book describes how the Covid-19 pandemic revealed stunning inequities and inefficiencies in the US healthcare system which existed for far too long. This national emergency has forced a rapid acceleration in reimagining and implementing a seamless system of integrated, digitally enabled health services that are decentralized and personalized to patient needs. Dr. Nundy provides a compelling blueprint for reengineering today's medical practice with the tools of technology while addressing the critical sociocultural determinants that dramatically affect patient care. He explores this once-in-a-century opportunity to redesign America's healthcare system with technological innovations and transformational approaches so that it focuses on the patient, moves care from the hospital to the home, and emphasizes the power of prevention to effectively address Covid-19 and the many other healthcare challenges and opportunities that lie ahead.

—Rear Admiral Susan Blumenthal, MD, MPA (ret.),
former US Assistant Surgeon General and Clinical
Professor at Tufts and Georgetown University Schools
of Medicine

CARE
AFTER
COVID

WHAT THE PANDEMIC REVEALED
IS BROKEN IN HEALTHCARE AND
HOW TO REINVENT IT

SHANTANU NUNDY, MD

New York Chicago San Francisco Athens London Madrid
Mexico City Milan New Delhi Singapore Sydney Toronto

1 2 3 4 5 6 7 8 9   LCR   26 25 24 23 22 21

ISBN   978-1-264-25912-0
MHID   1-264-25912-3

e-ISBN   978-1-264-25913-7
e-MHID   1-264-25913-1

Library of Congress Cataloging-in-Publication Data

Names: Nundy, Shantanu, author.
Title: Care after Covid : what the pandemic revealed is broken in healthcare and how to reinvent it / Shantanu Nundy.
Description: New York : McGraw Hill, [2021] | Includes bibliographical references and index.
Identifiers: LCCN 2020055086 (print) | LCCN 2020055087 (ebook) | ISBN 9781264259120 (hardback) | ISBN 9781264259137 (ebook)
Subjects: LCSH: Health care reform—United States. | Medical care—United States. | Telecommunication in medicine—United States. | COVID-19 (Disease)—United States.
Classification: LCC RA395.A3 N86 2021 (print) | LCC RA395.A3 (ebook) | DDC 616.8/31—dc23
LC record available at https://lccn.loc.gov/2020055086
LC ebook record available at https://lccn.loc.gov/2020055087

*For my daughters, Asha, whose name
means "hope" and who carries ours,
and Leela, "divine dance," who keeps us
on our toes and enjoying every moment,
and for Sonali, who means everything*

CONTENTS

PART III

DECENTRALIZED

ACKNOWLEDGMENTS

This book was made possible by three groups of people—those who shaped me, those who worked alongside me to build the solutions in it, and those who helped me write these pages. I'll work my way backward.

To the third group: you can't write a book in the middle of the pandemic with a full-time job and a busy clinical practice without an incredible team of people who lift you up and help you manage the day-to-day. I'd like to thank my editor, Casey Ebro, and the team at McGraw Hill for lending me their wisdom from building one of the best healthcare business categories in the industry. I'd like to thank Sara Camilli, a nurse by profession and an agent at heart. When we first chatted, I told Sara that for this book to work, I needed it to be a labor of love and a source of joy, and she delivered on both. I can't express enough gratitude to my collaborator, Beverly Merz. In addition to her sharp pen, she brought decades of experience questioning and examining the healthcare system as well as boundless energy to a project that we both saw as our chance to help fight this pandemic. I'd also like to thank Samantha Steinmetz, my research assistant, who, among other things, made sure that every chapter had an unrelenting focus on addressing health disparities.

I'd also like to thank my early readers, Mickey Chopra, Jumana Qamruddin, and my father, Rajiv Nundy, as well as give a special acknowledgment to Prabhjot Singh, who provided a firm, guiding hand through my early moments of peril in attempting to write this book. My thanks also to Kavita Patel, with whom I wrote a series of op-eds at the start of the pandemic, which became the genesis of this book, and Marty Makary, who provided critical insights and much needed laughter throughout the process.

I'm also deeply indebted to the individuals who generously offered their time in the midst of a pandemic to be interviewed for this book and fact check the content: Michael Barnett (Harvard School of Public Health), Lisa Cooper (Johns Hopkins), Renee Dua (Heal), David Horrocks (CRISP), Sam Inkinen (Virta), Jonathan Jackson (Dimagi), Ali Khan (Oak Street Health), Joe Kvedar (Mass General Brigham), Bruce Leff (Johns Hopkins), Reza Manesh (Northwestern Medicine), Ateev Mehrotra (Harvard School of Public Health), Marc Rabner (CRISP), Rahul Rajkumar (Blue Cross Blue Shield North Carolina), Debbie Rogers (Praekelt Foundation), Sharmistha Rudra (Children's Hospital of Pennsylvania), Mark Sendak (Duke University), Bimal Shah (Teladoc Health), Kevin Volpp (University of Pennsylvania), James Wantuck (PlushCare), Saul Weiner (University of Illinois at Chicago), and Julie Yoo (Andreessen Horowitz). I would also like to thank my colleagues and patients who allowed me to share their stories. I've done my utmost to do so accurately and without revealing any identifying information, but acknowledge any errors as entirely my own.

To the second group: many of the ideas in this book come from a myriad of opportunities I've been given to attempt to make healthcare better and from the people who worked alongside me to see them through.

I'd like to thank my aunt, Hansa Nundy, and my uncle, Pradeep Dwivedi. When I was a freshman in college, still a teenager, they gave me the opportunity to volunteer in the village of Sonamukhi in West Bengal, India. A month-long visit to teach English turned into a three-year effort to build a school-based clinic—my first foray into distributed care—and a lifetime of lessons in what it means to live one's life in service to others.

At John Hopkins, I'd like to thank Peter Pronovost, Chris Goeschel, and Marty Makary. Although I was not yet even a doctor, they gave me my first chance to improve healthcare at scale, building checklists to reduce medical errors in the intensive care unit and operating room, and eventually sent me to the World Health Organization to implement their ideas globally.

At the University of Chicago, I thank "Mom" and "Dad": Monica Peek, who showed me how research can change the lives of our most vulnerable patients, and Marshall Chin, who taught me how to ask the right questions. I'd also like to acknowledge my partner in this work, Jonathan Dick, who deserves most of the credit for my first success in digitally enabled care.

From Evolent Health, I'd like to thank Frank Williams and Tom Peterson, who gave me my first real job. This was my first adventure in the healthcare industry and attempt at decentralized care, and I had an opportunity to learn from an incredible cast of characters: Anita Cattrell, Dan Durand, Eric Fennel, Seth Frazier, Jesse James, Kevin Maher, Nupe Metha, and many others.

At the Human Diagnosis Project, I'd like to thank my friends Jay Komarneni and Irving Lin. Their inspiring mission to build "one open system for all humankind" has forever pushed me to dream bigger in my work. I'd like to thank my all-star team (Joaquin Blaya, Tyler Brandon, Seiji Hayashi, Marc Rabner, and Kaeli Yuen), the earliest members of our global physician community (Leo Kao, Sandeep Palakodeti, Zaven Sargsyan, Kevin Shenderov, and Stephanie Sherman), and our nonprofit board and supporters (Rich Baron, Don Berwick, Dave Chokshi, Sanjay Desai, Gurpreet Dhaliwal, Harvey Fineberg, Sandeep Kishore, Mike Klag, Urmimala Sarkar, and Daniel Wolfson).

At the World Bank, I thank my colleagues and mentors Mickey Chopra, Tim Evans, and Muhammed Pate. Mickey's decades of experience in post-apartheid South Africa and at UNICEF and relentless focus on improving the health of mothers and children in the poorest communities in the world inspired me to join the World Bank. I quickly found kinship in a small but mighty team—Joaquin Blaya, Liza Mitgang, and Jumana

Qamruddin—whom I'm thankful to continue to collaborate with today.

At Accolade, thank you to the entire management team, staff, and most especially, our frontline care teams—our medical directors, nurses, pharmacists, behavioral health specialists, and health assistants—who put our members first every day and make my job as chief medical officer look easy. I'm deeply grateful to Mike Hilton and Rajeev Singh for giving me the opportunity of a lifetime, for their friendship, and for being the kind of leader that I aspire to be. A special shout-out to the "Nundy mafia"—Greg Burrell, Epson Chiang, Lisa Gardner, and Sean O'Donnell—the ones really driving the healthcare reinvention I talk about in this book.

This book has also been shaped by my clinical career—by my colleagues who've shown me how healthcare is supposed to work and by my patients who give this work meaning and urgency. Becoming a doctor requires thousands of hours of training, but sometimes forgotten are the thousands of people—doctors, nurses, pharmacists, social workers, patients, and families—on the other end of that training. The names are too many to list here, but if you're reading this, I remember you and I carry your lessons with me.

To my patients, starting from when I was a medical student to today, thank you for allowing me into your lives, sharing your stories with me, and for the incredible privilege of being your doctor. Thank you for the holiday cards, for humoring me when I take out photos of my kids, and for trusting me with your health.

I would also like to give my appreciation to frontline health workers everywhere. I often tell people that I'm not a real doctor because I only see patients one day a week. The real doctors and the real healthcare workers are the ones who care for patients every single day—five or six days a week—even when it's not glamorous, even when it's not easy, and yes, even when they have to put their own lives at risk. Your service astounds and inspires me.

Finally, I would like to try to thank the people in my life who make all of this possible. I thank my grandparents—my two grandfathers and my four grandmothers—who left their homes in India to start a better life. I thank my aunts and uncles who helped raise me and my cousins with whom I explored the creek behind our house. I'm also grateful for the family I've added along the way—the Rudra, Sanyal, and Lad families.

I thank my best friends—Joaquin Blaya, Jonathan Dick, Manish Gaudi, Tony Leung, Naveen Michaud, Kaunteya Nundy, Nitya Nundy, Sanjay Sankappanavar, Rishab Toteja, and Yajur Shukla—for their unfailing support and friendship.

I'd also like to thank the Paul & Daisy Soros Fellowship, which supported my medical school education and gave me a community to belong to.

I owe everything to my parents, Anju and Rajiv. Whatever they had, they gave to my sister and me first. I owe as much to my older sister, Neeti, who I'm always proud to say had a huge hand in raising me.

Thank you to my little ones, Asha and Leela, who I hope will one day read this and forgive me for often sneaking away from them to do my "BW" (boring work). In those very early mornings, when I would force myself to get up and write, when I almost considered giving up, what kept me going was peering into your bedroom and asking myself, "But what if this book could help them one day?"

Finally, I thank my wife, Sonali Rudra. This book and everything I do is as much because of you as it is because of me. You are an incredible mom, loving partner, and always the first doctor of our home. Thank you for making my normal these past 20 years together better than I could ever possibly deserve.

INTRODUCTION

In March 2020, just as the first cases of the new coronavirus, Covid-19, were spreading across the United States and before millions of Americans began sheltering in place, I flew to San Francisco to meet with a promising startup company. In my role as chief medical officer of Accolade, I was exploring new ways to bring telemedicine—patients seeing a doctor by phone or online—to millions of working Americans and families.

As the meeting wrapped up, the company's chief medical officer, James Wantuck, and I started talking shop about Covid-19. The United States had only a few hundred cases at the time, but it was already clear to us that a major pandemic was coming and that testing would be the linchpin of our national response. James was worried about how his patients without access to a brick-and-mortar clinic would get tested. In passing, he mentioned a laboratory in Washington state that was considering mailing test kits to patients so they could test themselves for the virus at home.

When I left the meeting, my mind was racing. At-home testing made sense. Although the coronavirus test requires advanced laboratory equipment to run, administering the test is very simple. I remembered doing my first swab for the flu as a medical student. I took a sterile cotton swab out of a plastic kit and gently pushed it into the patient's nostril until it wouldn't go any farther. I assumed I had done it wrong, but the nurse observing me assured me that I hadn't. If it was that easy to learn, patients could test themselves for Covid-19.

But then an even bigger idea occurred to me—one that could be a game-changer for my own patients back in Washington, DC, who were largely uninsured and often struggled with accessing care of any kind. If patients could test themselves at home, the entire care model for most patients with Covid-19 could be provided in the home, from triage, to diagnosis, to management, and finally, to recovery. For an infection that was expected to affect as many as 100 million Americans[1] and present mildly in 80 percent of them,[2] that meant up to 80 million fewer people showing up to hospitals and clinics for testing and care—and in the process exposing themselves, other patients, and healthcare workers to infection. It also meant more equitable access for individuals who too often are left out of the system—individuals who don't have a doctor, are uninsured or underinsured, live in poverty, reside in rural communities, and are racial and ethnic minorities.

As I headed back to the airport in an Uber, I found a crumpled boarding pass in my backpack and scribbled down how the process would work.

Step 1: A patient with symptoms or concerns of Covid-19 completes a self-assessment online.

Step 2: A doctor reviews the self-assessment and if appropriate, mails the patient a test kit.

Step 3: The patient swabs themself and ships the kit to a lab for processing, with results available electronically in 1–2 days.

Together with Kavita Patel, a physician at the Brookings Institution, I wrote a paper in the *Journal of the American Medical Association* in which we proposed at-home testing as an alternative to in-clinic and drive-through testing.[3] While drive-through testing was a critically important innovation, its major limitation was scale. Ramping up drive-through tests makes the most sense in densely populated areas, where hundreds of people can be served daily. However, we also needed to consider rural communities, where one in five Americans reside,[4] as well as people in nearly 10 percent of households without a car.[5] Drive-through testing still placed demands on healthcare professionals to administer the test and required investments to set up testing sites. In comparison, at-home testing could leverage the national postal system and private mail carriers and be run without staff. I followed up with opinion pieces in the *Washington Post*[6] and *Harvard Business Review*[7] and spoke with anyone who would listen—from policy experts to news reporters to healthcare executives—about the need to scale up home-based testing immediately. The response from doctors, patients, and business leaders was overwhelmingly positive. Their primary question was, "When will it be available?"

But the powers that be balked at the idea. Some were worried that the model would lead to overtesting. Others were concerned that patients wouldn't administer the test properly. Still others feared that care would somehow become less personalized or lower quality. Despite my assurances that test requests would be evaluated by a physician, that patients could be coached over video on how to administer the test, and that the model would strengthen—not replace—traditional medical care, the idea didn't take. Just a few weeks later, the US Food and Drug Administration (FDA) announced that at-home testing was not authorized.[8] I was massively frustrated. Although lack of test kits was still a major bottleneck, here was a pragmatic solution that could more efficiently and equitably distribute the test kits we had.

Over the next several weeks, more research was done that proved that at-home testing for Covid-19 was efficacious and led the FDA to reverse its decision. In June 2020, a major national laboratory company, LabCorp, began offering home-based testing. Soon other testing companies followed suit.[9]

But it was too little too late. Lack of testing had become a national embarrassment and the US epidemic was already well out of control.

○—○—○

This is a book about the future of healthcare, a future that Covid-19 has shown us we can't afford to keep getting wrong and that, in many ways, has already ushered in.

My aim here is to prepare you for the transformation now underway. Healthcare has changed more in the past several months than perhaps at any similar period of time in its modern history. Almost overnight, care has become more virtual, more home-based, and more patient-directed. These changes have profound implications for every stakeholder in the system. Understanding what this means for you and your organization is essential to succeeding in the post-pandemic world.

But at the same time, we've come up short. As shown in the opening example of at-home testing, we could have done much more to effectively respond to Covid-19. There is also more we can do going forward to address not only future pandemics but also mental health, diabetes, obesity, and the conditions that routinely impact our health. What we need now are fresh ideas and new thinking about how to tackle age-old challenges in our delivery system, including access, affordability, and equity. Covid-19 isn't just a once-in-a-century pandemic. It's a once-in-a-century opportunity to reinvent healthcare.

The future of healthcare, I argue here, is distributed, digitally enabled, and decentralized. To help you navigate the path forward, the book is structured around these three shifts. Each chapter starts with a vision of where healthcare needs to go, outlines what it will take to realize the vision, and offers a set of specific actions each major stakeholder in the system, including patients, can take to get there faster. But first, what do I mean by distributed, digitally enabled, and decentralized?

Distributed: Care will shift from where doctors are to where patients are—at home and in the community (Chapters 2 and 3). Healthcare will routinely be delivered virtually by phone and video, not only for urgent visits but also for primary care, chronic care, and mental health. In addition, doctor visits and even hospital-level care will increasingly take place at home.

Digitally enabled: Healthcare, and the relationships central to care, will be strengthened by data and technology (Chapters 4 through 8). Care will shift from siloed to connected, from episodic to continuous, from being between one doctor and one patient to more collaborative. It will move from one-size-fits-all to personalized. It will go from relying on the doctor's memory to being powered by data.

Decentralized: Decisions about care will more often be in the hands of those closest to care (Chapters 9 and 10). The power to determine who gets care and how they get it will shift away from governments and insurance companies to communities, employers, doctors, and ultimately, to patients and their families.

Together, these shifts present a framework to understand the new healthcare landscape and make strategic decisions that will impact you and your organization. During the pandemic, care became more distributed as many patients, for the first time, saw the doctor over the phone or video. It became more digitally enabled as many doctors began using text messaging and mobile messaging to communicate with patients between visits. It became more decentralized as the government ushered in a series of new regulations that made it easier for clinics to decide where and how to deliver care, including online, in the clinic parking lot, and at home.[10] But many of these changes were reactive. Had we more deliberately aligned our strategy with this framework, the outcome of this pandemic might have been much different.

This framework will be even more important in the post-pandemic world. What Covid-19 has brought into sharp focus is that our healthcare system is fundamentally flawed. This makes it not only maladapted to responding to pandemics but also to delivering routine preventive and chronic care. We don't provide care to patients where and when they need it. We don't leverage data and technology to strengthen healthcare relationships. We don't let frontline health workers decide how best to deliver care. The result is a system that is unaffordable, ineffective, and inequitable.

At the same time, the pandemic has been accompanied by a set of deeper cultural shifts that will continue to drive changes in the health system. Patients began to see clinics and hospitals differently—as places that may not always be safe. Doctors realized that much of patient care can be provided virtually and outside of a healthcare facility. Policymakers couldn't help but acknowledge that healthcare is deeply inequitable. Employers began to consider healthcare as essential to business continuity. Insurance companies realized that the traditional model of fee-for-service payment made healthcare less resilient. Regardless of whether individual policies enacted to respond to Covid-19 are reversed after the pandemic, these cultural shifts will likely remain and impact the healthcare system for decades to come.

The upshot is that the rules that have long entrenched the health system have been rewritten, and perhaps surprisingly, largely in a good way for patients. To take best advantage of it, all of us—patients, caregivers, doctors, healthcare professionals, health systems, employers, entrepreneurs, investors, and policymakers—need to understand this new landscape and change our behaviors and strategies accordingly.

I've spent the past 20 years straddling the old healthcare world and the more digital one we've been ushered into. As an undergraduate, I studied engineering at MIT. I went to Johns Hopkins for medical school and then got an MBA from the University of Chicago. I've worked at a series of startup companies in digital health, artificial intelligence, and population health; conducted research with and held positions at the World Health Organization, Centers for Disease Control and Prevention, and The World Bank Group; and taken care of patients in East Baltimore, the South Side of Chicago, and Washington, DC.

Today, I continue to do the same. Monday through Thursday, I'm chief medical officer of Accolade—a health technology company that helps millions of Americans get the most from the health benefits their employers provide. Each of our members receives access to a health assistant and a team of clinicians over the phone or using a mobile app who use data and software to help them navigate the healthcare system. Fridays, I practice primary care at a traditional, brick-and-mortar clinic that provides care to the underserved on the outskirts of Washington, DC.

As I write this, the pandemic is far from over. Eight billion people have just had their lives disrupted by a healthcare crisis. Millions have died. The prospect of reaching the other side only to find a healthcare system that is still too inaccessible, too wasteful, and too inequitable is almost unbearable to consider.

But there is reason for hope. This crisis has created a wedge for change. The pandemic has tapped the vein of heroism and ingenuity that drew me and so many of my colleagues to our calling. Out of this pandemic a new model for healthcare is emerging, one that is built around patients, enabled by technology, and driven by healthcare workers. We each have a role to play in the work ahead and a stake in getting it right.

Let's get started.

CHAPTER 1

COVID-19 AS A CATALYST

O n Tuesday, September 11, 2001, the world changed. The twin towers came down. The Pentagon was hit. First responders dug through the rubble searching for survivors. Universities and schools closed. The mood of the country and the world darkened.

Daily life changed afterward. Flying would never again be the same. We learned to take our shoes off going through security and not to expect warm hugs at the gate. We routinely open our bags for guards at museums, sports events, and concerts.

Americans also changed. We were forced to acknowledge that *safety* is a relative term—we are all vulnerable—and that we are in this together.

On Wednesday, January 22, 2020, the world changed again. The United States confirmed the first case of the novel coronavirus on US soil.[1] Within two months, coronavirus, officially SARS-CoV-2, spread across the country. Universities, schools, and businesses closed. Millions of Americans started working from home. Hospitals and intensive care units (ICUs) in major hot spots like Seattle and New York City overflowed with patients. Test kits and surgical masks to protect healthcare workers were on back order. Toilet paper ran out.

Although the pandemic is not yet over, it's already clear that healthcare will not go back to the "old normal." But the question is what should the "new normal" look like? This question is essential if we hope to mitigate the next pandemic and improve the day-to-day experience of care. To answer it, we need to start by understanding what made Covid-19 unique and why our healthcare system was so poorly prepared to respond to it.

WHAT MADE COVID-19 UNIQUE

As the first cases of Covid-19 reached the United States, I needed to understand what was going on and what to expect. As chief medical officer of Accolade, I had to develop a strategy for our 1,200 employees spread across four geographic areas—Philadelphia, Seattle, Scottsdale, and Prague. I also needed a strategy for our customers—large and small employers, including healthcare systems, major airlines, and retailers, for whom we provided healthcare navigation services. I also needed to get up to speed to take care of my own patients and to respond to my family and friends, who were already starting to call and text, asking whether they should seek medical care for flu-like symptoms, travel for work, or cancel their summer vacations.

The first weekend in February, I hunkered down in my basement office for a crash course in Covid-19. In the 15 years since I had started my medical training, the world had dealt with several major epidemics—H1N1, Ebola, and SARS. I needed to understand what made Covid-19 so different from other viruses and what that meant for how our health system needed to respond. I read every research study and report on the virus I could get my hands on. I emailed colleagues whom I had worked with at the World Health Organization, the Centers for Disease Control and Prevention (CDC), and the World Bank. Over the course of the weekend I came to realize why Covid-19 would pose a unique challenge to healthcare systems globally.

The Extent of Asymptomatic Spread

Individuals without any signs or symptoms of Covid-19 can carry the virus for days and still transmit it to others, and even remain asymptomatic for the entire course of their infection.[2] This meant that we couldn't simply rely on people's symptoms to know when to isolate them to break the chain of transmission. Moreover, for those who became symptomatic, the symptoms were largely indistinguishable from other flu-like illnesses, making it nearly impossible to know from symptoms alone if someone had Covid-19.[3] Testing would be essential to diagnosing Covid-19 and tracking the spread of infection. It dawned on me that our ability to scale up testing to reach everyone who needed it would determine the success or failure of our response. Knowing that access to healthcare was already a problem for far too many people, I could see that we had our work cut out for us.

The Extent of Severe Cases

Although estimates varied, early reports suggested that 20 percent of those infected developed severe respiratory symptoms requiring hospitalization and 1 to 2 percent of patients died.[4] These rates were even higher in older adults and individuals with chronic conditions such as type 2 diabetes.[5] The high rate of severe cases meant that hospitals, which typically operate at or near capacity worldwide, would quickly become overwhelmed. Worse, as places that already are known as breeding grounds for infection, hospitals would also become sources of spread among patients and healthcare workers. It also meant that individuals with poorly controlled chronic diseases—the elderly, the poor, and the disenfranchised—would suffer disproportionately.[6] Because healthcare systems are weakest in disadvantaged communities, reaching those areas—which our health system has never managed to do well—would be essential to our response.

At the same time, because younger and healthier people were less likely to be severely affected, they might be less likely to practice prevention than they were during the Ebola epidemic, which had high rates of mortality across the age spectrum.[7] This meant that a strong public health response to prevent the spread of infection in younger people would be imperative. And yet this too is often where our system fails.

Widespread Disruption to Routine Care

The need to slow the spread of infection, as well as the heightened—and often well-founded—fears of getting infected in a hospital or clinic, would cause many people to stop or delay seeking medical care. This would mean widespread disruptions to preventive and chronic care. At the same time, the need for these services would be greater than ever. Chronic conditions would be exacerbated by the social determinants of health—as businesses closed or slowed down, joblessness and financial insecurity increased, and food security became more of an issue—and mental health would worsen due to widespread fears and social isolation. We already had data from the 2014–2016 Ebola epidemic suggesting that such widespread disruptions to routine care could lead to as many deaths as the pandemic itself.[8] I realized that we would be dealing with two pandemics at once: first, the infection itself and second, the increase in chronic disease and mental health issues, what I later defined in a paper with my colleagues Manmeet Kaur and Prabhjot Singh as "the second hit" of Covid-19.[9] The dual pandemics would require the health system to be responsive and agile enough to shift care to where it was most needed. Unfortunately, *responsive* and *agile* are probably the last two words most people would use to describe the healthcare system.

In short, Covid-19 was the perfect storm—a virus almost perfectly engineered against not only the human body but also the way we humans had designed our healthcare systems. It was an infection that spread as fast as H1N1, caused as much death as SARS, and disrupted society as much as Ebola.

If we had any hope of containing this pandemic, we needed a new health system—and fast.

TWO STEPS FORWARD

Elements of that new health system came sooner than I could have possibly imagined.

A few weeks into the start of the US pandemic—on a crisp, sunny March morning—I drove into my clinic in Washington, DC. Aside from the empty roads, it seemed like a normal day. But when I got inside, instead of being greeted with a busy waiting room, I was handed a clinic smartphone. Almost overnight our clinic had put in place a new protocol: every patient had to be "seen" virtually first. Afterward, if the patient appeared to be free of Covid-19 and needed to be seen in person they could be scheduled for a face-to-face visit.

In the 10 years I had been practicing medicine, I had never done a patient visit over the phone or by video. I wasn't sure exactly how it'd work, but I soon found out.

My first patient, whom I'll call Ms. Emilia, was 39 years old. The electronic health record told me she needed to be seen for "fever/body aches × 4 days." When I dialed her number, Ms. Emilia immediately picked up. "This is Dr. Nundy from the clinic," I said in Spanish. I almost reflectively followed with "What brings you in today?" before settling on "My nurse asked me to call you for a visit."

If Ms. Emilia shared my hesitation with virtual care, she did not show it. She jumped into her story: She had body aches for the past four days and a fever the previous night. Her boyfriend had gotten sick three days before she had, and she was worried they could have Covid-19.

Although I wished I could check her oxygen level and examine her, I couldn't and likely didn't need to. She had no shortness of breath or cough and no chronic health problems to speak of. I ordered a Covid-19 test. Three hours later, through my clinic window, I saw her minivan pull up to the clinic parking lot—our makeshift drive-through testing site. Soon one of my nurses, in blue mask and face shield, walked over to her car to administer a nasal swab test. Two days later, her Covid-19 test came back positive. Shortly thereafter she fully recovered.

Within weeks, what would have seemed impossible just months earlier had become routine. Our clinic, like many around the country, went from 0 to 70 percent virtual visits. We had trained all of our frontline care teams on new protocols and set up a drive-through testing site. But perhaps most important, we had upended ingrained workflows and thrown many of our deeply held assumptions about where and how healthcare needed to be delivered out the window.

Although the shift to virtual care was a bright spot, it became clear, as Covid-19 wore on, that these innovations were falling short.

HOW COVID-19 EXPOSED DESIGN FLAWS IN HEALTHCARE

Any hope of containing this pandemic would require a superbly functioning health system. But instead, we had a system that failed us in many respects. Some failures were related to the interference of politics, others to widespread mistrust of science, and still others to lack of public health capacity and pandemic preparedness—issues that are beyond the scope of this book. But chief among the many failures is how healthcare is fundamentally designed.

Lack of Access to Medical Care

Perhaps more than anything else, lack of access to testing became symbolic of our failed Covid-19 response. There wasn't enough testing capacity. There weren't enough laboratories to run Covid-19 test samples. There weren't enough test kits and test supplies.

But lack of access to testing was also indicative of a deeper design flaw in our healthcare system—lack of access to medical care. Far too many people today lack access to affordable healthcare. They are uninsured or underinsured, live in communities without enough doctors or that are mistrustful of them, or face financial or logistical hurdles to seeing one. They are disproportionately poor, come from racial and ethnic minority groups, and live in rural areas.

In short, inadequate testing was just the symptom; lack of access to care was the disease.

Overreliance on Doctors

Early in the spring of 2020, as the first wave of the pandemic was hitting hard in my community, nearly every patient I saw was for Covid-19. Over video or telephone, I would ask them a series of questions: What symptoms do you have? Cough? Fever? When did it start? Any known exposures to Covid-19? Any difficulty breathing? Because Covid-19 was so prevalent and the symptoms so nonspecific, I would inevitably order a Covid-19 test for nearly every patient who called. It occurred to me that I was serving a function that could just as well be handled by a nonphysician or an online self-assessment.

It's not that I minded these calls. In fact, quite the opposite. It felt personally rewarding to help my community in a time of need. What concerned me was the inadvertent harm. Requiring every patient to be seen by a doctor created a bottleneck to testing and care. Only patients who had a doctor and could afford to be seen by a doctor received care. I was also concerned about the opportunity cost. Instead of managing the crush of routine Covid-19 patients who didn't need the expertise of physician, I could have instead focused on helping higher-risk patients with Covid-19 or patients who needed care for their chronic diseases. Not for the first time in my career as a physician, I felt frustrated because I couldn't reach the patients who needed me most.

Overreliance on Clinics

As more care became virtual, much of clinic-based care was exposed as unnecessary. The check-in usually performed at a front desk could be done over the phone. Time spent in a waiting room certainly had no value. Routine physical exams for healthy individuals—something we've known for years are usually unnecessary—were abandoned, even when visits were in person.

During the pandemic we learned that often the safest, most efficient place to get care for Covid-19 was outside of a clinic, through a combination of virtual visits and drive-through testing. But in most clinics, this innovation wasn't extended to other health conditions. By and large, patients with preventive and chronic care issues still had to come to a clinic to receive comprehensive medical services and, as a result, many didn't.

Overreliance on Hospitals

Early in the spring, when New York City became the epicenter of the US epidemic, the world was horrified by scenes of overflowing hospitals, stories of families not able to be at their loved ones' bedsides, and cases of patients dying at home of treatable heart attacks and strokes for fear of catching Covid-19 in the emergency room.[11]

It became clear that hospitals and emergency rooms were, by design, maladapted to the challenge of Covid-19. Because hospitals are expensive to operate, they need to run at or near capacity, which makes it difficult for them to operate at surge capacity and accommodate more patients. Moreover, hospital care often requires doctors and nurses to go directly from one sick patient's room to another, increasing the risk that they will become infected themselves and spread infection to others. Hospitals by their nature bring thousands of people into the same physical location, which also makes them potential breeding grounds for infection. Yet, even though hospital-level care can be provided safely in people's homes, during the pandemic hospitals seemed to be the only places where patients with more acute health issues were being treated.

Lack of Systems for Chronic Care and Prevention

During Covid-19, preventive and chronic care declined precipitously. Screenings for common cancers like breast cancer and colon cancer plummeted.[12] Childhood vaccination rates declined markedly.[13] Primary care visits were down by 60 percent.[14]

Part of the problem is that healthcare is reactive by design. Healthcare is designed around visits to doctors, even though patients live with their heart disease or diabetes year-round. We wait for patients to schedule an appointment and then we address their health needs. When a patient stops taking their medication or when their blood pressure or blood sugar levels shoot up, we often don't know about it. It has always been a challenge to get patients to come in for recommended tests like colonoscopies and mammograms and routine follow-up visits for their chronic conditions, but the pandemic magnified the problem. The system isn't set up to anticipate their needs and reach out to them proactively.

Lack of Attention to Mental Health

Covid-19 also exposed flaws in the mental healthcare system. Widespread fears of the pandemic, mounting political and social turmoil, profound social isolation, and calamitous financial difficulties all conspired to create what some have called the "epidemic within the pandemic"—a mental health crisis. Many people already lacked access to mental health services and the increased demand placed a strain on the short supply.[15]

At the core of the problem is the long-standing separation between physical health and mental health. Many primary care providers lack adequate training in mental health issues, and medical care in general overly focuses on the biomedical aspects of care to the exclusion of social, environmental, and mental health needs. Moreover, mental healthcare remains highly stigmatized. As a result, although many people were getting care for Covid-19, the toll of the pandemic on their mental health was largely ignored.

Inadequate Investment in Primary Care

Like most of medicine in the United States and around the world, primary care is paid on a fee-for-service basis, meaning that doctors get paid for visits and specific services. Doctors typically don't get paid for providing care over the phone or providing transportation for patients, and they have no pool of dollars that they can use to invest in surgical masks or gloves, build a drive-through testing site, or purchase technology or software to enable them to switch to virtual care.

During the pandemic, clinics like mine logged 30 to 40 percent fewer visits, which meant 30 to 40 percent lower revenues. At the same time, most independent practices operate with only six to eight weeks of cash on reserve. In the midst of the pandemic, primary care—the bedrock of a functioning healthcare system—came to the brink of collapse.

Massive Disparities in Healthcare

As declared most aptly by Dr. Martin Luther King Jr., "Of all the forms of inequality, injustice in health is the most shocking and inhuman."[16] Perhaps more than anything else, Covid-19 impressed in the minds and hearts of people everywhere just how inequitable our health system is. It seems almost ironic now that in the early days of the Covid-19 pandemic people were calling it the "great equalizer."[17] In theory, Covid-19 was a disease anyone could get—it wasn't confined to a handful of countries or only the poor. Indeed, many of the first people in the United States to get infected were frequent travelers—celebrities, basketball players, and business leaders who jet from meeting to meeting.

But very quickly, like most other health conditions, Covid-19 became a disease of the disenfranchised. We started seeing alarming rates of Covid-19 in African American, Latino, and Native American communities. By April, African Americans made up about 30 percent of the infections and nearly 33 percent of the deaths, even though they comprised only 13 percent of the population.[18] By May, Native Americans made up 57 percent of cases compared to being 9 percent of the total population in New Mexico, and 30 percent of cases compared to being 2 percent of the total population in Wyoming—a trend that was replicated on a national scale.[19] It was a double hit. Black and brown individuals got Covid-19 more often. And when they got Covid-19, they got much sicker from it.

The reasons were multifactorial. For one, underserved communities were at greater risk of exposure. They could not shelter in place as easily. Many were still going into work every day—stocking grocery stores, picking up garbage, and boxing items that we ordered online—while white-collar professionals transitioned from the office to working remotely from home. Even when these essential workers got sick, many had to keep working and exposing others because, for them, there was no such thing as paid time off. Moreover, they weren't able to self-quarantine effectively. In my clinic, which cares for a largely underserved immigrant community, I saw whole households become infected—grandparents, aunts and uncles, parents, children, newborn babies. It wasn't that they weren't willing to comply with self-quarantine recommendations; it was that they couldn't.

Their households consisted of 10 or more people living in a space that in a wealthier neighborhood might be occupied by a family of 4.

Second, individuals with chronic diseases like diabetes and high blood pressure had significantly higher rates of serious illness and death from Covid-19 than those who didn't. Again, for a number of reasons—food deserts, lack of safe places to exercise, unstable housing, transportation barriers, poor healthcare coverage, and lack of healthcare providers—African Americans, Latinos, and Native Americans not only have higher rates of these conditions but are less likely to have these conditions under control.[20]

Finally—as the wave of Black Lives Matter protests during the height of the pandemic illuminated—all of the health issues affecting underserved communities are exacerbated by systemic racism, not only outside the walls of healthcare but shockingly within healthcare too.[21] As just a single data point from the pandemic, African American patients with symptoms of cough and fever were less likely than white individuals with the same symptoms to be given a test for Covid-19.[22]

COVID-19 AS A MAGNIFYING GLASS

The inadequate US response to Covid-19 shocked the world time and again. People were in disbelief that so many Americans couldn't get access to testing, and that healthcare was so much worse for racial and ethnic minorities. But to many healthcare insiders, Covid-19 wasn't an anomaly. It was a magnifying glass.

Just a handful of statistics illustrate the sorry shape of US healthcare before Covid-19:

- Routine healthcare is far too inaccessible. An estimated 20 to 40 percent of Americans do not have a primary care physician, the provider for most healthcare services. That number has only increased in recent years.[23]

- We recognize serious and chronic health conditions too late. There are 165,000 people in the United States with HIV who do not know they are infected.[24] One in five Americans with diabetes are unaware that they have it and often have had the condition for years before diagnosis.[25] One-third of breast cancers are diagnosed at a late stage.[26.]

- Hospitals are unsafe—not just during a pandemic. Each year 1.7 million people get an infection from a hospital and 99,000 die.[27] Medical errors account for another 250,000 deaths in hospitals.[28] They stem from a range of issues—blood clots because patients are kept in beds too long, falls because they are overmedicated, and medication errors due to understaffing.

- We tend to overlook prevention. Study estimates show that only 37 percent of adults get the flu vaccine,[29] and rates of appropriate cancer screening for breast cancer, cervical cancer, and colon cancer range from 60 to 90 percent.[30] Just as 66 percent of people don't exercise,[31] 75 percent don't follow healthy diets,[32] and nearly 38 million Americans still regularly smoke cigarettes.[33]

- Healthcare is deeply inequitable across multiple dimensions.

  ○ *Mortality:* For more than a century, research has shown that African American and Native American individuals have a shorter life expectancy than white individuals.[34] African American women are three to four times as likely to die from pregnancy-related issues than are white women, and African American infants are more than twice as likely to die than white infants are.[35]

○ *Morbidity:* In the United States, African Americans are 60 percent more likely than Whites to have diabetes and twice as likely to have preventable complications when they have it.[36]

○ *Quality of care:* African American women with symptoms of pre-eclampsia during pregnancy are less likely to be taken seriously and suffer a higher rate of complications.[37]

A CHANGE IN MINDSET

Covid-19 not only highlighted the flaws in the health system, but also created a sea change in the way we view healthcare—what we expect from our health system and how care is delivered. That shift will persist well beyond the pandemic and have far-reaching effects on the system. We have come to a few realizations:

Care Doesn't Have to Happen in a Clinic or Hospital

During Covid-19, patients came to realize that hospitals and clinics are not the safest places to be. They learned that healthcare does not necessarily require being there in person. Because many had no choice but to access care virtually, they came to understand firsthand that healthcare can still be as empathetic and personalized over the telephone or by video as it can be in person. They also realized the tremendous ease of access and convenience that virtual care affords. No more waiting weeks for an appointment, taking a day off work, spending an hour in a waiting room—all to see a doctor for less than 15 minutes.

For their part, doctors, many of whom practiced virtual care for the first time during Covid-19, discovered how much care can be provided online. In medical school, we are taught from day one about the sanctity of the "history and physical" in which the patient describes their symptoms and medical conditions and the physician examines them. In a virtual world it's just the history with no physical, and most of us were pleasantly surprised to discover that we could manage 50 to 80 percent of our patients just as well by telephone or video alone.

The biggest shift during Covid-19 was that patients and doctors came to trust care provided outside of a clinic or hospital. A mentor of mine once told me that "medicine moves at the speed of trust." Perhaps more than issues of technology, payment, or workflow, it was doctors' and patients' reluctance to trust virtual and other forms of care outside of a clinic or hospital that had been holding us back.

Technology Can Help Extend Care Beyond Visits

Once I was issued a clinic iPhone and permitted to text message and FaceTime with my patients, I suddenly found myself keeping up with them more. I'd call them the day after a visit to see how they were feeling or shoot them a text and see if they got the medication I had prescribed. Most of the time they replied that everything was fine. But sometimes it turned out things weren't fine and reaching out to them allowed me to course correct sooner than I would have otherwise.

Technology also made navigating the healthcare system simpler for patients. Early in the pandemic, I had a patient who was Covid-19 positive and needed a medical letter for work. But how would I get him a note if, because of the risk of transmission, he wasn't allowed to come inside our clinic? I could mail it to him, but that would take too long. I couldn't fax it to his boss because I was no longer coming into the clinic every day and—it being 2020, after all—I didn't have a fax machine at home. Instead, I wrote a letter on my computer and texted him a photo of the letter, which he, in turn, texted to his boss.

Technology supported behavior change, too. At Accolade we designed a daily check-in for individuals whose workplaces were still open. Using a mobile app, they would record their symptoms and exposures, and if everything checked out, be cleared to come in to work that day. Part of the idea was to catch Covid-19 early and keep infections out of workplace. But part of it was a behavioral nudge, reminding people to maintain social distancing and prevent infection in the first place.

Prior to Covid-19, doctors, patients, and the policy community had soured on digital technology after bad experiences with electronic health records and excessive hype around mobile apps, big data, and artificial intelligence. During the pandemic, we learned that the right role for technology in healthcare should be simply to increase the "care" in "healthcare."

Care Decisions Should Be Local

During Covid-19, we renewed the idea that care is local and that the responsibility, resources, and authority to make care decisions should be in the hands of those closest to care.

As the pandemic hit, clinics and doctors needed to respond—and quickly. They started making decisions and shifting resources in ways they never had before. What made this rapid response possible was not only necessity but also deregulation—the relaxation of restrictions on telemedicine and the use of FaceTime, WhatsApp, and nonsecure means of communication with patients, as well as the ability to reimburse for virtual visits and practice across state lines.[38] This allowed each clinic to decide how best to respond to the pandemic given the resources they had available and the needs of their individual communities. Some like mine used FaceTime and WhatsApp to conduct virtual visits, while others purchased specialized software. Some set up their own drive-through testing sites and negative pressure isolation rooms to examine Covid-19 patients,[39] while others redirected all Covid-19 patients to places that could more safely handle Covid-19 so they could focus instead on delivering routine preventive and chronic care.

This shift to localized care decisions extended beyond the walls of the healthcare system. Local governments and public health agencies began to exercise more authority, as they decided where to setup testing sites, whether to institute sheltering in place measures, and how to reach vulnerable health populations. Businesses made more local decisions, too, about whether to remain open or shift employees to remote work. Many employers launched their own pandemic response teams. At Accolade, our response team met daily for the first three months of the pandemic. As chief medical officer, I'd begin each meeting by reporting out on the latest epidemiology—how many new cases there were nationally, where the hot spots were—and the latest CDC, state, and local guidelines. Next, we'd discuss whether and how Covid-19 was affecting our business operations. Finally, we'd plan our communications—blogs, videos, email campaigns—to keep our employees informed and up to date on the latest guidelines and internal policies. In many organizations, these teams took on even greater responsibility. When it became clear that the public health system did not have sufficient resources to do contact tracing, many employers took it into their own hands. Some even purchased their own test kits and hired nurses to administer them.[40]

Perhaps the most dramatic shift was with patients. We became more aware of our bodies—our breath, our hands. We washed our hands more regularly and were more mindful of what we touched. When we went to the grocery store, we were careful about every step, every wipe of disinfectant. What became deeply ingrained in our minds was: my fate is in my hands, literally.

THE WAY FORWARD

During Covid-19, we saw the seeds of change sown and the early sprouts of a new health system better adapted to the needs of patients. But without nourishment, the progress we've made will wither away, and we risk falling back to the same system that we had before the pandemic, with the same failures that Covid-19 magnified.

Covid-19 was the catalyst for change, but to what end? What is our vision for a more effective, efficient, and equitable health system? And what is our path to realizing it?

The answer is a healthcare future that is distributed, digitally enabled, and decentralized—a future that Covid-19 has shown us is urgently needed and has also accelerated us toward.

We begin by reexamining the old notion that healthcare needs to happen in a clinic or hospital and envisioning how care can be reinvented to begin at home.

PART I

DISTRIBUTED

magine waking up one morning with pain in your right side. You go to the kitchen for a glass of water. Drinking it doesn't help. You think about what you ate last night, but you didn't have anything unusual.

It's getting worse. You try a heating pad, but it still feels like someone punched you in the stomach. So you use a phone app to ask your health provider what to do.

Someone immediately messages back with a series of follow-up questions. After providing more details on your symptoms, you get a phone call from Monica, who identifies herself as a nurse navigator. Monica picks up where the messaging system left off.

You haven't spoken to Monica before, but she already has all of your health information pulled up—your medical record, insurance claims, employer benefits, and previous interactions with the system. She can see that you're 42, are slightly overweight, and have diabetes, but you have no history of abdominal pain or gastrointestinal issues. She knows where you work, that you have two young kids, and that with your busy work schedule and family life, you prefer to receive care at home rather than in a clinic.

She asks you to check your temperature and your heart rate. You haven't had a chance to get one of those wireless devices that can transmit your vital signs automatically, but you have an old-school thermometer that you use for your kids and you know how to check your own pulse.

Your elevated heart rate has her pretty concerned, so she schedules you to see a doctor in the next hour. In the meantime, she advises you to not eat anything.

Twenty minutes later, you're on a videoconference with Dr. Jones. He has been your doctor for the last four years. Knowing you as he does, he can immediately tell that you are in significant pain. He assures you that he is going to get to the source of your problem soon. Based on what you told Monica, he thinks you may have gallstones or even appendicitis and wants you to get immediate medical attention. Normally, he would drive over to your home and examine you himself, but this time he's away at a medical conference.

You discuss your options: either go to the emergency room (ER) or have a paramedic come to your home. You don't have a sitter for the kids and don't want to bring them along to the ER, so you both agree on option two.

Within 30 minutes, a paramedic is dispatched to your home. She checks your vitals and examines your abdomen with a small ultrasound. The images are captured digitally and sent to a radiologist at the nearby hospital.

A preliminary read comes back within minutes. The paramedic hands you a tablet computer so your doctor can explain to you what's going on. Your ultrasound shows inflammation of the gallbladder wall due to gallstones, which are likely related to your weight and diabetes. You don't have any signs of serious infection, but he orders a set of labs to be certain.

The paramedic draws your blood, and on his way back to his dispatch unit he drops the sample off at a lab a mile away. Dr. Jones had ordered the labs "STAT," so they are processed the moment they arrive. The results, combined with your symptoms and ultrasound findings, confirm the diagnosis: acute cholecystitis. Fortunately, it was caught early. You will need intravenous (IV) antibiotics and fluids.

Together, you and Dr. Jones decide that you should be "admitted" to hospital-level care at home. Soon your home hospital comes to life. Within the next hour, a nurse arrives and a delivery service brings in a hospital bed, monitoring equipment, IV pole, and IV antibiotics. A few minutes later, you move into your new "hospital room."

A doctor with expertise in hospital care comes to check on you. She has already spoken to Dr. Jones and has reviewed your labs and ultrasound images. She helps explain your condition to you and your spouse. She emphasizes the need for surgery at some point to remove your gallbladder, but you decide to delay it for now. She lets you know that she will see you in person or over video every day while you are receiving hospital-level care and that she will keep your doctor in the loop.

The first night, a nurse stays by your side, monitoring you closely to see if your condition is worsening or if you need to be urgently transferred to a hospital. The second day, based on your improvement, the nurse comes for the day shift but leaves at night. On her way out, she reminds you that your phone is your "call button" and you can summon her or one of her colleagues at any hour.

A couple of days later, you're feeling better and your labs have improved. Your doctor decides to "discharge" you from hospital-level care. You shift to rehab care with physical therapists coming to your home to speed your recovery. Your family has been nearby the whole time.

By day four, you're fully discharged and ready to resume life as usual. You feel back to your normal self—except that you're now even more motivated to lose weight.

Although this example may sound like science fiction, it's not. All of the components are already in use. Nurse call centers that can be accessed by text or phone are widely available. Primary care models that combine clinic, home, and virtual care services are becoming more commonplace. And hospital-at-home is a safe and effective care model that is steadily gaining traction as an alternative to hospital care.[1]

In this example we can glimpse the near future—a future in which healthcare shifts away from hospitals and clinics and into homes, communities, and wherever patients are.

Distributed care is care that happens where and how it makes the most sense for patients. Rather than concentrating every visit, diagnostic test, and follow-up in facilities like hospitals and clinics, care is distributed across a broader range of sites, including people's homes, communities, and workplaces, both in person and online. Put more simply, as my sister, Neeti Sanyal, a global expert in design and healthcare, describes it, distributed care is the concept that "care happens where health happens."

Distributed care doesn't mean eliminating traditional health-care settings—far from it. Hospitals and clinics will continue to play a major role in healthcare delivery. People will still rely on these facilities for certain complex and acute care needs, but for most people they will become secondary, rather than primary, sources of care.

The most obvious benefit of distributed care is that by deliv-ering care closer to home and without the overhead costs of expensive medical facilities, healthcare will be more accessible and affordable. It also has the potential to be more effective and equitable. Our health is largely driven by our behaviors and our environment. By delivering care where we live and work, distrib-uted care can be more holistic and better address the root causes of poor health—including social isolation, poor nutrition, phys-ical inactivity, and mental and emotional distress. In addition, it can reach communities who live too far from the nearest clinic or hospital or who are too distrustful to step foot in one.

During Covid-19 we saw a major acceleration of this shift. Almost overnight, clinics like mine, which had previously relied exclusively on in-person visits, went virtual. And Americans, for the first time, got medical tests outside of clinics and emergency rooms, at drive-through testing sites that popped up around the country.[2]

But distributed care can go much further than this. Had healthcare been more distributed prior to the pandemic, we would have been better prepared for Covid-19. By deliver-ing more care outside of healthcare facilities, we would have reduced the spread of Covid-19 in hospitals and clinics—better protecting both patients and healthcare workers—and avoided overflowing hospitals. By having a comprehensive way to deliver routine care virtually and at home, we would have prevented widespread disruptions to routine vaccinations, cancer screenings, and primary care.

The next two chapters envision the shift to distributed care. Chapter 2 details how care will increasingly be delivered virtually—by phone or video. Chapter 3 describes how more healthcare services—from lab tests and doctor visits to hospital-level care—will be delivered at home.

CHAPTER 2

VIRTUAL

CONNECTING DOCTORS TO
PATIENTS WHEREVER THEY ARE

A few months into the pandemic, I saw a patient I'll call Mr. George, who taught me both the promise of virtual care as well as its limitations. Mr. George was a 55-year-old gentleman who had suffered a stroke a month earlier. It had left him with some paralysis on the right side of his body as well as difficulty speaking. Although he had a major stroke, he had not seen a doctor in the three weeks since his discharge from the hospital. That was alarming! It meant that no doctor had followed up with him to see how well he was recovering from the stroke or to arrange for the physical therapy and speech therapy he needed. No one had even checked his blood pressure or ensured that he was on the right medications to prevent a second stroke from occurring. The problem, I later learned, was that Mr. George couldn't make it in to see his old doctor. He didn't have a car, and after the stroke was no longer able to take the bus.

When he called my clinic to find out if we were taking new patients, our front desk staff alerted me to his situation and arranged for a virtual visit. Within an hour, I was on the phone with him, helping him sort out his medications—it turned out that he was taking a couple of them incorrectly—and counseling him on warning signs of another stroke.

While we were talking, I looked up his address online. To my delight, he lived just a block away from another one of our clinic locations. I notified my nurse, and she set him up with a new primary care doctor, whom he was able to see the next day and has followed up with regularly since.

○—○—○

This chapter is about the shift toward *virtual care*, which I define as medical care between a doctor and a patient provided live over a phone or computer instead of in person. This definition excludes self-service patient apps, remote monitoring, email, and other asynchronous (not occurring in real-time) ways of interacting with a doctor. These are covered in Part II of the book. I purposely use the term "virtual care" rather than "telemedicine," which is an industry term that has largely come to refer to standalone companies that provide virtual care and often connotes urgent care services rather than comprehensive care, which is my emphasis here.

For Mr. George, the ability to see a doctor by phone shifted the frontlines of care from the clinic, which was hard for him to get to, to where he was. If my clinic hadn't implemented virtual visits because of Covid-19, Mr. George would probably not have seen a doctor that day and perhaps not until he had another stroke. Virtual care isn't just a more convenient and efficient way to deliver care; it is a lifeline and a front door for patients who otherwise might not have care at all.

At the same time, Mr. George had needs that went beyond what I could provide virtually. He needed a doctor to examine his right side and ensure his strength was improving. He needed a nurse to sort through his pills and help him understand what each medication was for. In addition, as someone who hadn't had regular medical care in a long time and potentially didn't trust the healthcare system, he may have needed or simply preferred a doctor whom he could sit down with face-to-face and build a relationship with. He couldn't necessarily do this via video call either, because he didn't have a smartphone or access to high-speed internet at home. As a result, it was imperative that I, his virtual care doctor, was connected with a brick-and-mortar clinic so we could get him the in-person care he needed.

VISION OF VIRTUAL CARE

The virtual care I envision is one in which care is available where and when patients need it, is provided by someone they trust, and is seamlessly integrated with their overall healthcare.

The gallbladder story embodies this vision. You, the patient, were able to speak to a nurse within minutes and a doctor within an hour. You didn't need to schedule an appointment. You didn't need to drive yourself to a clinic. You didn't need to sit in a waiting room where you'd expose yourself and others to infection. The doctor you saw was one you already knew and trusted. He had access to your complete medical record, so he understood the full context of your medical needs. Your doctor was also able to virtually coordinate all of your care, from sending a paramedic to your home, to ordering blood work and much more. Had he been in town that day, he would have seen you in person as well.

According to many observers, Covid-19 accelerated the shift toward virtual care by 7 to 10 years.[1] During the pandemic, virtual care, which had long been relegated to the edges of medicine and used primarily for urgent complaints, suddenly became mainstream. For a brief period of time, during the peak of the pandemic, almost half of patients were relying exclusively on virtual care.[2] Patients didn't use it only for colds and coughs. They also used it for primary care, chronic care, mental health, specialty care, and even for ancillary care like physical therapy.

However, as the use of virtual care exploded, the experience for many patients didn't always resemble the seamless experience of the gallbladder story. Often patients saw a different doctor each time. The doctors didn't have access to patients' previous medical histories. The doctors were unable to order lab tests or refer the patient to in-person care. Care was often solely focused on the acute issues and was not comprehensive. We also realized that many patients were being left behind—those without computers, smartphones, and access to high-speed internet.

It may be helpful to consider an analogy. Many people have likened the shift to virtual care to banking. In the past, we did all of our banking in a brick-and-mortar bank. Then we started doing a number of our transactions at an ATM outside of a bank. And today we increasingly do our banking online—even transactions like depositing a check are now possible with a snap of a photo. When we make an online transaction, use an ATM, or visit a bank, we think of all of those things simply as banking. We don't think of banking virtually versus banking in person. For most of our needs, online banking is sufficient, and it's usually the starting point for our transactions. At the same time, there are people who will always prefer to go to a physical bank, and that's OK too.

Similarly, pre-Covid-19 most of us received our medical care in a brick-and-mortar clinic. During the pandemic we shifted some of our testing to drive-through sites and standalone laboratory centers (our equivalent of an ATM). And going forward, those who prefer it will increasingly do our routine medical care online or by phone.

But now imagine if every time you log in to your bank account online, you were asked to estimate how much money you had available for withdrawal. Or when you deposit money at the ATM you have to send a fax to your bank so your account can be credited. That would be absurd! But in fact, during Covid-19, that's how many telemedicine companies operated. They didn't have your medical information, they didn't share records with your primary doctor, and they weren't integrated with the rest of the healthcare system.

THE ADVANTAGE OF VIRTUAL CARE

When we settled into the "new normal" of the pandemic, I saw the kind of patient that I previously would have assumed would not be well served by virtual care. On my schedule was a 24-year-old woman I'll call Ms. Gabby, who had scheduled an appointment for anxiety. Reviewing her record beforehand, I learned that she had recently given birth to a healthy baby, but otherwise had no history of depression or mental health issues. I took out my clinic iPhone and called her over FaceTime video.

As soon as she picked up, I could tell she had been crying. As we talked, she explained her situation. She had recently been exposed to Covid-19 at work and was worried that she might have it—and worse, pass it on to her family. She was a single mother and was largely on her own to care for her baby. When she became pregnant her mother had agreed to help her with the baby, but social distancing had prevented her from doing so. I could see that Ms. Gabby was scared, lonely, and tired.

To my surprise, I found the call curiously intimate. In many ways, talking over video created a safe space for her, allowing her to open up more than she might have in person. I also felt more comfortable. I found myself sharing my own concerns about Covid-19 and struggles with the new normal—things that I typically don't do in person.

As we talked, her spirits began to lift. Simply having a healthcare professional to talk to seemed to help. I also was able to screen her for postpartum depression and convince her to meet with our clinic social worker. At the end of the call, she thanked me profusely.

When I hung up, it struck me that without access to virtual care, the visit might not have happened at all. After all, the logistics of getting to a clinic with a newborn baby—in between diaper changes, breastfeeding, and naps—is hard enough, let alone in the middle of a pandemic. And I suspect that, as with many patients with mental health concerns, the social stigma associated with her condition may have created another barrier.[3]

Greater Convenience and Access

The most obvious value of virtual care is the convenience and the accessibility it offers. No longer will patients have to take time off work, wait weeks for an appointment, and spend an hour in a waiting room just to see a doctor for a few minutes. They'll be able to access a doctor when and where they need one and on their own terms.

This greater convenience is important in itself, but as Ms. Gabby showed me, the benefit goes beyond convenience. It means that patients will access care when they otherwise wouldn't. This is particularly true for our most vulnerable patients—the elderly, individuals living in poverty, individuals with disabilities, and racial and ethnic minorities—those who often need care the most. For these patients, the logistical and financial barriers to accessing care can be insurmountable. For many of my patients, coming to see me in clinic often means losing a day's wages and arranging for costly childcare and transportation.

Virtual care also has another advantage over facility-based care—increased privacy. Receiving care for mental health issues, sexual and reproductive health, and HIV/AIDS carries significant stigma that can impede access. For Ms. Gabby, simply having to check in with a front desk clerk for a visit for "anxiety" may have been enough to deter her from seeking care.

The impact of virtual care on these barriers became evident during the pandemic when I called my colleague, Dr. Michael Barnett, a primary care doctor in Boston, to compare notes on what we were seeing in our respective practices. Like mine, Michael's clinic serves the traditionally underserved. And like me, Michael knows that 10 to 20 percent of his scheduled patients don't make it to their appointments. But during the pandemic, both Michael and I saw our no-show rates plummet to nearly zero. Why? Because virtual care had removed the barriers. "When you're doing telemedicine, everyone shows up because they're all available by phone, and they don't want to turn down the chance to see the doctor, even if they've forgotten they have an appointment," Michael said.

More Effective In-person Care

Virtual care also has benefits for patients who need in-person care. In my clinic, virtual care became a kind of "forward triage" system—a model that is increasingly called "virtual first." Rather than automatically scheduling every patient for an in-person visit, we saw patients virtually first, and then if we needed to see them in person for a specific physical exam or test, we had them arrange for a face-to-face visit.

During the pandemic, I found that two-thirds of my patient visits could be managed completely virtually. But even for the one-third who needed in-person care, I seldom found the virtual visit to be a waste of time. If patients were on multiple medications, I'd ask them to bring their medication bottles to clinic so I could make sure they were taking them correctly. If patients had back pain, I'd advise them to try ice and ibuprofen for a few days first, so I'd have a sense if a conservative approach to treatment might work. For those who needed blood work, I'd send them to the lab first, so that I could walk them through the results when they came to see me in person.

Greater Personalization

Virtual care, and in particular video visits, can offer a window into the home and lead to a better understanding of patients. During the Covid-19 pandemic, Leela, my four-year-old daughter, had her annual well-child visit, which we did via video for the first time. A key component of these visits is to assess a child's development: at age two, they should be able to jump in place, build a tower of four or more blocks, and use two-word phrases; at age four, they should be able to hop up and down on one foot, draw a square, and tell a story.[4] Normally at these visits, Leela is quite shy, clinging to her mom or me and refusing to talk to the doctor. This time, in the security of her own home, Leela was a chatty Cathy. When her pediatrician asked her whether she could build a tower, she ran into her playroom and came back with a princess castle she had built with Legos, excitedly telling the doctor what each part of the castle was and the names of each color she used.

I also saw the value for patients with chronic conditions. Managing heart disease and diabetes can take a village. With virtual care, the village was able to more easily be a part of the visit. Patients increasingly brought family members, friends, and formal caregivers—people who normally would have to take time off work or rearrange their schedules—to their visits by having them simply appear on camera or dial into a virtual visit.

Patients were also able to connect to a doctor anywhere in the country. No longer were they limited to the physicians in their geographic area. They could be seen by doctors who have a specialized interest or experience in exactly the condition that they had or by doctors who aligned with their personal needs and preferences—for example, for non-English-speakers, physicians who spoke their native language, or for LGBTQ individuals, doctors who themselves are from the LGBTQ community. The ability to connect with doctors across distance also impacted the millions of Americans living in medically underserved areas—places without enough doctors and clinics to accommodate everyone who needs care.

LIMITATIONS OF VIRTUAL CARE

Virtual care had its benefits, but it also had important limitations. The first, perhaps most obvious, is its very nature—it's not hands-on. Early in the pandemic, I saw a patient who I suspected had Covid-19. But based on the symptoms she described over the phone—fever, runny nose, mild cough—I thought that it would be sufficient for her to get care virtually and get tested at our drive-through testing site. Fortunately, when she arrived, they not only tested for Covid-19 but also checked her oxygen level. It turned out her oxygen level was below 88 percent—the danger threshold. We got her to the emergency room right away and she was admitted to the hospital. Fortunately, she made a speedy recovery. In an in-person world, 100 percent of my patients with respiratory viral symptoms would have their oxygen level checked along with their heart rate, blood pressure, and weight, as part of the routine check-in process.

With virtual care, there isn't a readily accessible way to check a patient's blood pressure and heart rate, conduct a physical exam, perform diagnostic tests and blood work, and do minor procedures like wrapping a knee brace or lancing a boil. This limitation isn't a problem in itself. Virtual care isn't intended to replace in-person care, just as care in a clinic isn't intended to replace care in a hospital. The problem comes when virtual care isn't seamlessly integrated into in-person care and care begins to default to being all virtual, even when additional services are needed.

Second, virtual care risks becoming less comprehensive and lower quality. Consider this scenario: A woman who is recently diagnosed with high blood pressure develops urinary frequency. She knows that frequent urination can be a sign of a urinary tract infection (UTI) and that UTIs are common in women her age. It's the weekend, and her doctor's office is closed, so she contacts a telemedicine service. Based on her symptoms, the doctor prescribes an antibiotic. The doctor doesn't have access to her prescription records, and she didn't think to tell him that she started a new blood pressure medication. Had he known, he would have suspected that she was experiencing a common side effect of her new medication, a diuretic, and not have prescribed an antibiotic she didn't need.

Third, virtual care risks leaving behind individuals who need care the most, the elderly and the underserved. Many such patients face three overlapping barriers to accessing virtual care: access to a computer or smartphone, high-speed connectivity, and digital literacy. A 2018 study of Americans over age 65 found that a third lacked a home computer with high-speed internet, a third didn't have a smartphone with a wireless data plan, and a quarter lacked both.[5] Lack of access to connected devices is also common in rural and minority communities and in households living in poverty. In addition, many individuals face barriers to using technology, including not knowing how to use a computer, difficulties with language and literacy, and physical conditions such as arthritis, visual impairment, and hearing loss.[6]

MODELS OF VIRTUAL CARE

To take advantage of the promise of virtual care while addressing the limitations, a number of new models of healthcare will emerge.

Primary Care

Primary care is defined by what legendary Johns Hopkins researcher Dr. Barbara Starfield called the four Cs:

1. *Contact:* your primary care doctor is the first person you contact whenever you have a health concern.

2. *Comprehensive:* your primary care doctor cares for all of your family's needs, including preventive care, chronic care, and mental health.

3. *Coordinated:* your primary care doctor coordinates all aspects of your care, including medications, specialist visits, and hospital care.

4. *Continuous:* your primary care doctor follows you longitudinally across your entire care journey.[7]

Often, the simplest way to think about primary care is to imagine living in a small town in the 1950s. You have one doctor who sees you for all of your family's medical needs. She's your doctor, your therapist, your pharmacist, and maybe even your marriage and family counselor. She lives in your community. She was the first doctor you saw for everything because she was the only doctor in town. And she had a very flexible model of care. Sometimes she would see you in her clinic. Other times she'd see you at home, or she would just run into you in the grocery store and ask you how you were doing.

Although we still cling to this ideal vision of primary care, for the vast majority of Americans, it is only an ideal. We don't come close to achieving Dr. Starfield's four Cs. Even for patients who have a primary care doctor, much of the care they receive isn't with that doctor. When they get sick, it may be hard to get an immediate appointment with their primary care doctor, so they often go to an urgent care center and see a different doctor, which fails to satisfy Dr. Starfield's first C: first *contact*.

When they do get in to see their primary care doctor, their visits are rushed. Increasingly, visits are squeezed into 10- or 15-minute increments, which is hardly enough time to get to know patients and provide care that is truly *comprehensive*.

Often when they get care from a specialist or are admitted to the hospital, their primary care physician is the last to know. Their care isn't *coordinated*.

When patients move or change insurance plans, they often have to get a new primary care doctor, so care isn't *continuous*.

Virtual care has the potential to bring us closer to how primary care should work. For some patients who see a doctor in a brick-and-mortar clinic like mine, virtual care can extend their doctors' reach into their lives. I saw this firsthand during the pandemic. The ability to provide care virtually meant patients had near on-demand access to care. Instead of waiting for an appointment, they often could have the initial visit on the same day or even within an hour. That meant that I could be my patients' first *contact.* Even if they needed to go to the emergency room, I knew about it and could help prepare them for what to expect, so care could be more *coordinated.* For many of my patients, it also made it easier to follow up with me a week after a visit to see how they were tolerating a new medication or to see how their symptoms were resolving, so *continuity* improved. It also created more space to get to know them outside of a hurried and stressful clinic and more in their natural environment, which made care more *comprehensive.*

For other patients—particularly those who live in a community without enough doctors or who struggle to make it to a brick-and-mortar clinic because of distance or logistical barriers—an even bolder idea is to do away with the physical doctor's office completely. I talked to Dr. James Wantuck to learn exactly how such services deliver comprehensive primary care. James is chief medical officer and cofounder of PlushCare, a startup company that has provided primary care to tens of thousands of patients completely virtually.

Here's how it works: Patients schedule their first visit using a mobile app. Not surprisingly, many of those visits are for an urgent complaint and patients are seen on demand. Following their first visit, patients receive a comprehensive assessment to complete online, in which they provide their full medical history, their preventive healthcare, and their medications. Based on the exceptional care they receive during their first visit, three-quarters of patients complete that assessment, and a substantial percentage of those subsequently sign up with PlushCare for primary care. Patients then pay a monthly subscription fee for access to a primary care doctor who will schedule video visits with them and to a care team that they can message with for support between visits.

All PlushCare visits are done through video and often with the same doctor. They have an electronic medical record that tracks patients' lab results, medications, and preventive healthcare needs. It even makes recommendations to doctors for care patients may be missing, such as diagnostic tests and cancer screenings. They also have a system for ordering lab tests at local testing centers and for referring patients for in-person care. The system is integrated with both of the national private labs— Quest Diagnostics and LabCorp—so PlushCare can seamlessly access and share patients' test results.

Specialty Care

Although seeing a specialist like a cardiologist, oncologist, or surgeon often involves tests and procedures that can only be done in person, a surprising amount of specialty care can also be provided virtually.

For example, my wife is just about as specialized as they come. Sonali is a breast radiation oncologist. She only sees cancer patients, only those with breast cancer, and only for treatment with radiation. While much of the care Sonali provides centers around administering radiation—which needs to be done in person and typically in a hospital—a significant portion of her care is amenable to virtual care, as she learned during the pandemic. While patients wanted to discuss their initial treatment plan in person, many preferred their follow-up visits—each of which adds to the burden of living with cancer—to be virtual. What Sonali found is that once a caring and trusting relationship is built, virtual care can extend this relationship.

During the peak of the pandemic, Sonali was doing 20 to 30 percent of her visits virtually. Not surprisingly, doctors whose specialties are more "cognitive" have been able to do an even greater percentage of their visits virtually. For example, studies show that 80 percent of dermatology visits[8] and rheumatology visits can be managed virtually.[9]

Mental Health

During my conversation with Dr. Michael Barnett, the primary care doctor in Boston, I was surprised to hear Michael, who is usually very measured and understated, describe mental health as "the killer app for telemedicine." But I quickly realized that he was right.

Michael summed it up perfectly for me: "Mental health is the sector of healthcare that has transitioned over to virtual care most seamlessly. There is something fundamental in the act of conversation and listening that can be done virtually." He elaborated that mental health visits don't rely on a physical exam, but on verbal communication—relaying emotions and ideas. Mental health also requires frequent, often weekly, interactions for months on end, which are easier to do virtually. Virtual sessions also offer privacy for patients who don't want to be seen going to a therapist's office.

Michael also sees virtual care playing a greater role in a critical area of mental health—addressing addiction. In his other role as a health services researcher at the Harvard T.H. Chan School of Public Health, Michael has been studying the role of buprenorphine and other medication therapy in addressing the opiate crisis. Prior to the pandemic, federal regulations prohibited physicians from prescribing buprenorphine virtually unless they had seen the patient in person first. Patients on methadone were required to visit a clinic every day to receive their dose. Once the risk of spreading Covid-19 through clinic visits became apparent, regulations were relaxed, enabling outpatient services to deliver prescriptions remotely—and expanding treatment options greatly.

Expanding options is key to treating addiction, Michael says. "In addiction treatment, the overall goal is harm reduction. We're trying to engage as much of this population—which is, by nature, difficult to engage—as possible. I wouldn't say that my first choice is virtual care, but for many patients, if you insist on an in-person visit, they won't come at all. For others, if you insist on a virtual visit, they won't engage. But the more options we have, the better."

REALIZING THE VISION

How do we realize the vision of care where and when patients need and want it, and yet is comprehensive, integrated, and inclusive?

Currently, much of the focus is on technology-only solutions. There are devices that will measure your blood pressure and heart rate and wirelessly transmit that information to the doctor. There are even ones that will allow you to simulate a doctor's exam by enabling you to examine your heart or your lungs, or to look into the ears of an infant child for signs of an infection.

But when I asked both entrepreneurs and policy experts what they considered key to delivering quality care virtually, no one mentioned a technological tool of any sort. In fact, they all gave me essentially the same answer James Wantuck did—building trust. I naturally wondered how it was possible to build trust without having a face-to-face interaction. "That was actually the hardest thing we had to do," James says.

He told me that when he cofounded PlushCare the first patients weren't—as he had anticipated—millennials who were well off, tech savvy, and accustomed to doing everything online. Instead, they were people in medically underserved areas like rural communities who couldn't find a doctor—many who needed to be convinced they could trust a physician they never met in person.

The PlushCare team did a lot of work upfront to create trust online. They posted their pricing and privacy policies prominently on their website. They only interviewed physicians from the top 50 US medical institutions and screened for qualities like empathy and warmth before they hired them. But just as important, they made the patient's introduction to the doctor highly personal. They made doctors' photos, personal information, and patient ratings available on their mobile app before they even asked users to provide so much as an email address. And once a

PlushCare member has selected a doctor, that doctor is the one they generally see going forward. The result: "Patients tell us they feel listened to and heard."

In addition to building a trusting relationship, virtual health-care should also provide the following:

- Whole-person orientation. In every visit, even if it's for something relatively minor like an upper respiratory illness, the physician should take the opportunity to educate the patient on prevention or at least connect that patient back to their usual care provider for those services.

- Dedicated doctors and care teams. For any virtual care service that provides longitudinal care, giving patients access to the same provider is essential—whether by phone, online chat, or video visit. Doctors and care teams need to be employed by or at least spend a significant por-tion of their time on the service to maintain continuity with patients, and the service needs advanced scheduling systems so that follow-up appointments can be with the same providers whenever possible.

- Access to patients' health information. Today, many telemedicine services that are accessible through people's employers or direct-to-consumer lack this critical capa-bility. When their healthcare providers see a new patient, they don't have any of the patient's prior health informa-tion and, worse, some don't even maintain the records of patients they have previously seen.

- Integration with in-person care. Virtual care providers should have clear protocols for when remote visits should be followed by in-person visits or in-person services like lab testing and X-rays. Ideally, they should coor-dinate care with brick-and-mortar clinics and facilities to provide a seamless care experience, regardless of a patient's needs.

- Accessibility by diverse populations. Patients face a number of barriers to virtual care that these services need to be explicitly designed to overcome. For example, for elderly patients, Northwell Health, New York's largest healthcare provider, dispatches healthcare workers to patients' homes to help them get set up for their initial virtual visit.[10] For patients with physical limitations, it may make sense to have a nonphysician healthcare worker in the home for all the visits to serve as the patient's eyes, ears, and hands. For individuals who lack device access or high-speed connectivity, virtual care may need to meet patients where they are technologically. In my clinic, many of my patients don't have smartphones or computers, so we connect by telephone. In other cases, program sponsors may need to invest in device access and internet connectivity. In the post-Covid-19 world, digital access will increasingly equate to healthcare access.

STRATEGIC ACTIONS

Post-Covid-19, consumers and employers will increasingly demand virtual care options across the continuum of care—from urgent care to primary care to mental healthcare to specialty care—all of which need to be seamlessly integrated with in-person care and the overall care experience. Virtual care has the potential to improve health disparities for those who face the greatest barriers to care—individuals living in poverty, the elderly, and the marginalized—but it also risks exacerbating disparities if not explicitly designed to address the three overlapping barriers to virtual care: lack of digital literacy, access to devices, and high-speed internet connectivity.

Organizations that move quickly to provide virtual care and do so in a way that strengthens relationships between patients and doctors and drives better outcomes will be well positioned to succeed. Organizations that don't adjust fast enough will be left behind.

To take best take advantage of this shift to virtual care and position yourself and your organization for success, here are some steps each stakeholder can take.

Patients, Caregivers, and Consumers of Care

- Seek out doctors and services that offer virtual care, especially if you have difficulty getting to a doctor's office. Virtual care options are available for a wide range of services, from urgent care to mental health to dermatology and cancer care.

- If you prefer virtual care, find a service that integrates with in-person care for when the need arises. Ask: Do you provide preventive and chronic care? Are you able to order lab tests and see my results? Will you coordinate my care with other doctors and specialists when needed?

- Do your part to ensure your virtual care is as comprehensive as possible. Consider buying basic medical equipment such as a scale, thermometer, and blood pressure cuff—they don't have to be fancy or expensive. If asked to fill out a questionnaire before a virtual visit, do it, even if you think your visit has nothing to do with your recent medical history.

Physicians and Healthcare Professionals

- Get trained on how to provide high-quality and effective virtual care. Virtual care is not the same as in-person care. It requires a different clinical workflow and new approaches for building trusting, empathetic relationships.

- Invest in a home or work office with a good camera and proper lighting. It helps! This is all part of the new "webside" manner that doctors and healthcare professionals need to master.

- Once the barriers to practicing across state lines are removed, consider offering your time to see patients in rural and low-income areas, who otherwise would not have access to your expertise and skills.

Healthcare Delivery Systems

This includes traditional clinics and hospitals and telemedicine companies.

- Extend virtual care beyond urgent care into nearly all aspects of care—particularly primary care and mental health. Ask yourself what site of care is best for each patient and then reorganize care to deliver it accordingly.

- Tightly integrate virtual and in-person care. Delivery systems that provide seamless integration across care sites and help patients navigate between online and offline care will have a competitive advantage over those that do not.

- Collect, track, and report data on multiple dimensions of quality. To compete, traditional health systems offering virtual care will need to measure wait times and patient satisfaction. Telemedicine companies offering comprehensive care will need to measure quality, cost, and outcomes.

Payers, Including Employers, Government Entities, and Health Plans

- Expand telemedicine coverage and benefits, particularly for primary care and mental health. In many cases, more than one telemedicine provider will be required to serve the full continuum of care.

- Reimburse telemedicine services fairly with payment equity—not payment parity—as the goal. Even better, move to risk-based payments, which I discuss in Chapter 9.

- Evaluate virtual care providers on multiple dimensions— not only on utilization rates, wait times, and patient satisfaction, but also on quality (such as chronic disease management, antibiotic appropriateness, and preventive health screenings), costs, and patient-reported outcomes. A simple rule is that quality measures for the same type of service should be no different between in-person and virtual care options.

- Consider investing in internet and device access, digital literacy programs, and language translation services to ensure equitable access to virtual care. For example, screen patients for low digital literacy at the point of care and use lay health workers to help them learn the basics of using a computer or smartphone device.

Policymakers

- Ensure payment equity, rather than payment parity, between traditional care and virtual care models, so that virtual care is neither artificially disincentivized or incentivized.

- Expand definitions of primary care, advance practice models, and medical homes to include virtual-only or virtual-first primary care models.

- Remove restrictions on licensure for medically underserved areas so that primary, mental health, and specialty care can expand to these areas virtually, including across state lines and even international borders. Better yet, enable a national telemedicine license so doctors can deliver virtual care anywhere in the country.

- Invest in broadband connectivity, digital literacy, and device access to ensure equitable access to healthcare. Consider public-private partnerships to improve computer ownership in rural and low-income communities (e.g., through computer donation) and improve telehealth participation through a combination of digital technology access, training, and coverage.

- Modernize privacy and security regulations so that technology does not serve as a barrier to the expansion of virtual care.

Healthcare Investors and Entrepreneurs

Invest in and build companies that:

- Are purpose-built to deliver virtual primary care and comprehensive care.

- Facilitate seamless transitions between online and offline care.

- Expand the capacity to manage urgent and chronic care conditions at home (e.g., connected physical exam devices, at-home testing).

- Facilitate new kinds of data exchange between traditional health systems and digital health providers.

- Are designed and proven to expand access to high-quality virtual care for vulnerable health populations, including individuals who have visual or cognitive impairments, lack connected devices or high-speed connectivity, or have low digital literacy.

Finally, although unrelated to virtual care specifically, we should all do whatever we can to achieve affordable, high-quality healthcare for all.

CHAPTER 3

HOME-BASED

DELIVERING CARE WHERE
PATIENTS LIVE

A few months before the Covid-19 pandemic, I finally got around to doing something that had been on my mind for some time—getting life insurance. It had been a few years since the birth of my first child, and every time I got on a plane to travel for work, I felt a gnawing anxiety about what would happen to my young family if the plane went down.

To qualify me, the insurance company needed to conduct a physical exam and blood work. But as a busy professional married to an equally busy professional, with one—and then two—kids, I just hadn't gotten around to it.

Then a friend suggested that I get my insurance exam at home, something I hadn't known was possible. A home exam had a lot of appeal. I often worked from home and wouldn't have to coordinate schedules with my wife to make sure someone was home with the kids. Now out of excuses, I made an appointment for an exam.

On the scheduled day and time, a kindhearted, middle-aged African American nurse, whom I'll call Ms. Graham, arrived at my home. Having never received healthcare services at home before and as someone fascinated by healthcare delivery, I tried to see the visit from her eyes: Driving to my home, she immediately gets a sense of the context in which I live—a suburban neighborhood of single-family homes on the outskirts of Washington, DC. As she turns onto my small street, she notices many of the yards strewn with tricycles and soccer balls. She walks up six stairs to my porch, and I welcome her into our home. On her left, she sees a series of maps—one for each of the cities where my wife and I have lived together: Boston, Baltimore, Chicago, and Washington, DC; on her right, my prize possession, a well-worn grand piano gifted to me by one of my favorite aunts when I completed my medical training. Heading down the front hallway, she runs into two of the three most important people in my life—my daughters Asha and Leela—already home from school and in their playroom coloring. She is seeing me in my natural environment—no hiding my dirty dishes or my kids' scribbles on the walls—and on my own terms, as a whole person and not simply as a patient in a gown.

From there on, the exam itself was comfortingly familiar. Just as we would in a clinic, we sat down, provider and patient. While I answered a series of medical questions, she entered the results into the electronic health system on her iPad.

Then came time for the physical exam. She checked my pulse and blood pressure. She asked me to provide a urine sample, which I did in the privacy of my own bathroom. She drew my blood as I sat at my home office desk. Then I lay down on my basement sofa so she could hook up a 12-lead and take my EKG—my first ever.

This simple encounter resonated with the vision I laid out in the gallbladder example earlier. I could see the benefits of home-based care. It was more convenient and more personal than clinic-based care.

I could also begin to appreciate the challenges. Coming into the home of a stranger, I learned, was no small feat. As we got to know each other and she learned that I was a physician, we exchanged "war stories" from our work. She told me about a time when she felt unsafe in a client's home and decided to cut the exam short.

There was also a logistical challenge. Having to contend with DC traffic—some of the worst in the country—she had to factor in the time of day, traffic patterns, and distance between her appointments, so she wouldn't be late for her clients and would arrive home in time to care for her grandchild. I began to appreciate that the barriers that I as a patient faced to get an exam were now shifted onto her.

She also had to be organized. She told me about times when she arrived at a client's home and realized she didn't have the right equipment—when the person she examined required a larger blood pressure cuff, or she ran out of vials for blood, or her iPad needed charging. For an insurance exam, these were minor nuisances and bad customer service at worst, but for acute medical care at home these issues could spell disaster.

This chapter is about the shift to *home-based care*, a form of distributed care we define as healthcare services—including primary care, urgent care, and hospital-level care—that are delivered in the home by healthcare professionals. Our definition excludes patient self-care, at-home testing, or other services performed by patients themselves at home. I discuss those in Chapter 10.

VISION FOR HOME-BASED CARE

The vision of home-based care is simple: the home is just another place for patients to get care and often the starting point.

Although home-based care is a vision of the future of healthcare, it also harkens back to a time when house calls were not innovative but routine, when doctors went from house to house, black bag in hand, caring for the sick and dispensing medicines.

It also has its foundations in public health—from mobile vans equipped with X-ray machines used for tuberculosis screening after World War II to community health workers in many low-income countries today who travel from household to household, administering vaccinations and diarrheal treatments.

Home-based care is making a comeback thanks to both a cultural shift and new technology. Patients have learned that clinics and hospitals may not always be the safest places to get care, an insight the pandemic further made evident. We've also found new ways to care for patients at home. We can now monitor and reach patients remotely using connected devices. We have software to manage logistics and supply chains to efficiently deliver goods and services to the home.

By caring for patients at home, we can have a better sense of a patient's social milieu—their home environment, family structure, and neighborhood—which studies show has a greater impact on their health than their biomedical context does.[1] We can dramatically expand access to care for patients, especially the elderly, people with disabilities, and people who lack transportation to visit their doctors, by bringing care to them rather than requiring them to always go to care.

Perhaps most important, we can renew the most essential element of care—trust—as I observed with my insurance exam. By the time Ms. Graham left, I felt in many ways that she knew me better than any of my doctors had in years. This is the ultimate vision for home-based care. Over the past few decades patients and doctors alike have bemoaned the deterioration in empathetic and trusting relationships that are central to care. In that brief interaction, I saw the potential for home-based care to reinvent those, too.

Home-Based Primary Care

In many respects, home-based primary care is a throwback to how healthcare used to be. Picture Dr. Marcus Welby, the fictional

1970s TV doctor of small-town America, who embodied the ideals of medical care for several generations. Not only did Dr. Welby have the perfect bedside manner, he made house calls. In many parts of the country, home visits are returning. Initially, these house-call programs were directed at the elderly and those with multiple chronic conditions. But more recently, they have been extended to younger and healthier patients, including children.

Dr. Renee Dua is the chief medical officer and cofounder of Heal, a company that provides home visits to families across the country with a staff of modern-day Welbys. I've been curious about what prompted Renee to leave a thriving clinical practice and embark on a startup, so I gave her a call. She explained that she got the idea after seven hours in an emergency room with her infant son. "As a doctor and mother, I shared the frustration of anyone who's ever waited three weeks for a doctor's appointment, sat in a germ-filled waiting room, or rushed to the ER because they had no other choice." She decided to reinvent the home visit for the twenty-first century.

This how the Heal model works: The doctor drives to the patient's home with a medical kit that includes everything that a primary care doctor would have access to in a clinic—from rapid strep tests, to wound care supplies, to vaccinations that are kept refrigerated. The doctor is accompanied by a medical assistant who performs blood draws, documents the encounter in an electronic health record system, and drives the doctor so he or she can spend time preparing for the next visit. A sophisticated software system schedules visits, enabling doctors to minimize their travel time so that they can spend more time with their patients. It's the modern-day black bag that Dr. Welby would be proud of.

Heal has expanded into Medicare, providing home healthcare for seniors. "There is a lot of parity between seniors and kids because they often aren't the ones making the decisions," Renee told me. She added that their caretakers—who are likely to be stressed out juggling work and home responsibilities—need a support system for healthcare, too.

She relies on Heal for her own family's healthcare. "I found that I need help with my kids, and I'm thankful that I have a system that supports me. The software we're building is caretaker oriented. It's full of reminders for caretakers as well as patients. In effect, it says, 'OK, Renee, your kids need their school physicals. Get them done.'"

In her own experience, the home visit is much less stressful than one in the clinic. Not only is it more comfortable and convenient, but also it is less anxiety-provoking. Kids, especially, are more likely to feel that they are in a safe space and as a result give their full attention to the doctor and to tests that require concentration, like hearing screening.

Renee is also keenly aware of the need to establish trust, so she takes pains to hire the right doctors. When she is interviewing applicants, she listens for three themes: "I want to spend time with patients. I'm tired of spending time on rigmarole. I don't want just to be in urgent care—I want to get to know my patients." If they don't express these sentiments, the process doesn't move forward.

Home-Based Acute Care

Home-based care isn't just a substitute for routine clinic visits. It can also substitute for urgent care visits and even the emergency room.

Home-based acute care can mean anything from taking X-rays when pneumonia is suspected to administering IV fluids for dehydration to providing respiratory support for chronic obstructive pulmonary disease (COPD). To deliver this level of care, providers bring some of the same equipment you'd find in an emergency room to the home. They also rely on virtual care to bring greater expertise into the home. One such company, Ready Responders, sends trained paramedics and emergency medical technicians to the home and patches in physicians via videoconference to help diagnose patients and determine the best course of treatment.[2]

Hospital-at-Home

Home-based care can be extended to hospitalization at home.

During the pandemic, hospitals were forced to contend with the surge of Covid-19 patients. They responded by cramming multiple patients into the same hospital room, erecting medical tents in parking lots, and converting empty hotels into make-shift hospitals.[3] Largely missing from this response was a far more humane and, in fact, evidence-based approach—hospitalizing patients at home.

To help cities like New York, my colleague Dr. Kavita Patel and I cowrote an op-ed in the *Journal of the American Medical Association* urging policymakers to immediately expand access. We used an example of a patient with congestive heart failure to describe how it could work.

Step 1: A patient presents to the emergency department for initial evaluation, including imaging and blood tests. If they require hospitalization, the emergency department staff consults with a hospitalist (a physician who primarily cares for acutely ill patients in a hospital setting).

Step 2: The hospitalist determines whether hospitalization at home is appropriate and, if so, coordinates the patient's transfer home, including arranging for a care team and the delivery of any necessary tests, drugs, or hospital equipment.

Step 3: The patient receives 24/7 nursing care and daily visits from a doctor through a combination of in-person and virtual care until they are ready to be discharged.[4]

Providing hospital-level care for patients with non-COVID conditions like congestive heart failure would reduce their exposure to Covid-19. The model could also be used for patients with Covid-19, provided that the home environment was conducive to self-isolation and family members could be adequately protected with personal protective equipment.

Some hospitals that already had hospital-at-home programs—most notably Mount Sinai Hospital in New York City—leveraged the model to transfer patients home sooner. In what they called "continuing hospital care at home," a patient admitted to the hospital for a typical four-day stay could be transferred to hospital at home after two days. Early release reduced their risk of exposure to Covid-19 and also freed beds, which were in scarce supply at the height of the pandemic.[5] Unfortunately, beyond a few isolated examples, the model didn't gain traction.

Realizing the Vision

The vision of patients being hospitalized and receiving more services at home is the dream and lifework of one of my mentors from medical school, Bruce Leff. Bruce is a geriatrician and health services researcher at Johns Hopkins and a pioneer of the hospital-at-home model. I called him to learn the story of the hospital-at-home movement and understand what it will take to distribute more care to the home.

Bruce was a newly minted geriatrician in the mid-1990s, making house calls to elderly patients who had mobility disorders and serious health issues that made it difficult to come to a clinic. In the course of these home visits, he'd sometimes encounter a patient with a urinary tract infection or pneumonia that required treatments like IV fluids and antibiotics that were typically administered in a hospital. However, when Bruce would suggest hospitalization, many of his patients were fearful of going, and some flatly refused. They had seen too many friends go to the hospital, only to come home more frail, more disoriented, and more sick—or worse, end up in a nursing home.

As a researcher, Bruce understood that while some of these feared complications were related to the illness that led to the hospitalization, others were in fact a result of the hospital stay itself. Around that time, *To Err Is Human,* a landmark report by the Institute of Medicine, exposed the public to the fact that hospitals are dangerous places, with deadly infections and high rates of medical errors. Moreover, it revealed that the dangers were higher for elderly patients, who risked becoming delirious and pulling out their IVs or falling and fracturing a hip.[6]

Bruce also knew that hospitals—with healthcare workers coming in and out day and night and constant noise from alarms and equipment—were far from comforting. As we often quipped during my residency training, "Hospitals are bad hotels." They may be needed for cures but are bad for healing.

So Bruce asked himself a simple question: Could patients actually receive hospital-level care at home? And he set about answering it.

He started by studying which patients could be safely and effectively hospitalized at home. He came up with four conditions: heart failure, cellulitis, pneumonia, and COPD. Then he developed criteria to help doctors decide when hospital-level care at home might be appropriate. Could you definitely diagnose the condition in an emergency room, clinic, or home? Was the patient's home environment safe and conducive for providing hospital-level services? His research found that a quarter to a third of patients with these conditions could be taken care of at home.[7]

Next, he did his "field of dreams" study. If he built a hospital-at-home program, would patients want it? Surveying a wide range of patients, he found that among elderly patients, a significant proportion would choose hospital-level care at home—confirming what he had heard from his own patients.[8]

When he was ready to put his idea to the test, he applied to do a small pilot study at his own hospital. The logistics of recruiting nurses, delivering hospital equipment, and setting up IV medications were easier than he'd anticipated. The hard part was getting approval from the hospital's institutional review board. His colleagues, despite being forward thinkers and researchers, didn't believe that the home was a safe place to deliver any kind of care, let alone to hospitalize patients. Bruce would encounter that objection time and again over the next 20 years. The biggest roadblock to home-based care wasn't technological. It was cultural.

After a successful pilot, Bruce and his colleagues proved the model in a series of larger and more scientifically rigorous studies. His research showed high rates of patients opting into the service and demonstrated that, compared to patients hospitalized for the same condition, they had lower mortality, lower rates of complications, higher functional outcomes, better caregiver experience, and lower caregiver stress. To top it off, healthcare costs were 30 percent lower compared with hospital stays.[9] As Bruce joked to me, if hospital at home were a drug, he wouldn't be here talking to me on the phone. He'd be somewhere in the Cayman Islands enjoying the spoils of a blockbuster innovation.

Patients want it and the research proved it works, so what will it take to make hospital-at-home and other home-based care a reality? Just a few things, Bruce says.

1. *Payment reform.* Governments, insurance companies, and employers by and large don't pay for care at home; they pay for care in clinics and hospitals. To fully realize hospital-at-home and other home-based care models, we need to reimburse healthcare providers fairly for providing care at home.

2. *Supply chain and logistics support.* When you practice in a hospital and you order an antibiotic, the antibiotic arrives on the floor in a few minutes. That kind of supply chain doesn't exist in the community or at home. Distributed models will only reach scale if healthcare providers can efficiently access the entire supply chain of nurses and other healthcare professionals, equipment, and medications required to provide care at home.

3. *Regulation.* We need a new set of regulations to enable healthcare professionals to care for patients at home while ensuring patient safety and minimizing fraud and abuse.

4. *Culture change.* In Bruce's words, "We need to start thinking about nonfacility care as good care."

Covid-19 has made Bruce particularly optimistic about breaking the last barrier, which has been the hardest to crack. Although doctors and healthcare researchers have known for years that hospitals are unsafe places, Covid-19 has brought that issue to the forefront.[10] At the same time, doctors and patients have begun trusting nontraditional care. They have experienced firsthand that you don't need to be in a hospital or a clinic to receive excellent care.

Bruce also sees how the benefits of hospitalization at home can be extended to younger patients, who also have a substantial risk of hospital complications. In addition, many of them would enjoy the convenience and comfort that hospital-at-home provides. I wish I'd been given that option a few years ago. My older daughter was born with a congenital problem that led to two hospitalizations before the age of three. The second time, she stayed in the hospital for an additional week just to receive IV antibiotics. Because of the risk of exposing other patients to her infection, she wasn't allowed to leave her cramped hospital room the entire time. It was miserable, and as parents, it pained us to see her suffer so much. Had hospital-at-home been available to us, we certainly would have opted for it.

Ultimately, Bruce's vision is of a world in which the home becomes just another place where care is seamlessly integrated. You see your primary care doctor at home. When you're sick, you get an acute-care visit at home. If you need to be admitted, you are enrolled in a hospital-at-home program. You have surgery at a hospital, but then you are directly discharged to hospital-level care at home. Even if you're initially admitted to a hospital, you can be transferred home after a couple of days to complete the rest of your recovery.

Forward-leaning health systems won't be able to do away with their hospital facilities—nor should they—but they can arbitrage their investments to decouple their services from the facilities themselves. Over time, hospitals should be able to reduce their facility-based imprint while actually expanding their reach to new populations.

In Bruce's words, "Once you start to create all of the pieces—all of these models that were developed as one-offs—you can start to put them together in a way that creates a whole home-based care environment that really keeps people away from the facilities. That to me is where this will all ultimately end up. And for organizations and entities that control the whole dollar and are at full risk, that's the direction they are going to want to go."

IMPLICATIONS FOR HEALTHCARE STAKEHOLDERS

The shift to distributed care will lead to what's referred to as the unbundling of care. As Julie Yoo, a general partner at the venture capital firm Andreessen Horowitz, explained to me: "[In the past] the only places we could go to get anything done were these monoliths called hospitals. Everything was centralized—whether it was low acuity or high acuity—everything was done in one place. Unbundling of care means that hospitals are going to shrink their services mix to the thing that it actually makes sense to do in a centralized and high-acuity way, and then everything else will be deconstructed at the edges and be made available to us in far more cost-effective ways."

Care concentrated in clinics and hospitals bundles services by default. You get all of your care in one place. When you go to the doctor's office, you're actually getting a number of different services combined into one. You are completing a health screening. You're getting your vital signs checked. You're seeing a doctor.

You're getting a physical exam. You're getting education and counseling. You're getting labs and other diagnostic tests. Distributing healthcare takes one or more of these components and delivers it separately.

The unbundling of care means that patients can access each component of care where it's best provided. It's the healthcare equivalent of cord cutting—getting rid of TV packages and choosing only the programs you actually watch. Like TV viewers who've canceled their cable service and are weighing whether to subscribe to Netflix, Disney+, or Hulu, those who purchase healthcare services—whether they are employers, payers, or patients themselves—will need to better understand the quality and cost of each one.

Unbundling will have the positive effect of increasing competition across the healthcare system. To compete, service providers will need to be transparent—providing price and quality data—and invest in improvements. It will also create opportunities for new kinds of providers that can deliver one or more components of care in more cost-effective ways.

Giving Patients More Options

An overarching concept of home-based care—and distributed care in general—is meeting patients where they are and how they want to be met. For some patients, that means much of their care will be virtual. For others—particularly older adults with multiple chronic conditions—care may still be predominantly provided in a clinic, with some components such as follow-up visits and routine blood work provided virtually or at home. Others will want or need to receive all of their care in a clinic or a hospital, as it is today.

Moving to a healthcare system that personalizes how care is delivered requires healthcare delivery organizations to understand the needs and preferences of their patients. It will also mean that clinics and doctors are empowered and given adequate resources to design care models that best meet their patients' needs. In other words, the healthcare system will need to become decentralized, a topic we'll dive deeper into in Part III of the book.

Optimizing the Physician's Time and Leveraging Virtual Care

The scarcest supply in healthcare is the physician. Care today is designed to optimize the physician's time. When we go to the doctor, we schedule an appointment that fits the doctor's calendar and we physically go to the clinic. Home-based care flips that model on its head, which means rethinking how physicians spend their time.

Having physicians travel from home to home can be costly. One approach to optimizing their time is what Dr. Dua described in Heal's home-based primary care model—having a medical assistant who drives the physician while the physician prepares for the next visit. Another solution is to make many of the doctor visits virtual. Medically Home, an organization providing hospital-at-home services, does this through mission-control-style command centers that enable a single doctor to virtually oversee the care of dozens of patients at once.[11]

Rethinking Supply Chain and Logistics

Healthcare delivery organizations have historically tackled the logistical challenge of healthcare—the "last-mile problem" of getting goods and services where they need to go—by requiring patients to come to them. The shift to home-based care will present a number of new challenges. How do you hire, train, and deploy healthcare professionals to deliver high quality care in the home? How do you deliver equipment, monitors, and supplies to patients when they need it?

It's not hard to conjure up a nightmare scenario in which an oxygen tank runs out in the middle of the night or a critical machine breaks down, and the system can't get the necessary equipment to the home fast enough. Delivering care at home may require an Amazon-scale delivery system on steroids.

Health systems will need to support patients in new ways. As more care is delivered at home, some of the burden of providing serviceable equipment to meet home-based care needs may inadvertently fall on the patient. Vijay Kedar, the founder of Tomorrow Health, a company that provides home-based equipment and services, describes a patient leaving the hospital with a list of medical equipment and supplies to buy. He has to contact a myriad of retail locations to get a CPAP machine, only to learn that there are a dozen types of CPAP machines with different clinical uses—some best suited for COPD, others for sleep apnea. In this new world, patients will need help navigating a range of different options, understanding their health insurance benefits and coverage, and coordinating between service providers. This process can be overwhelming, particularly for vulnerable patients who are still recovering from an acute illness. What they may need is a new kind of service to help navigate these options and more seamlessly coordinate these services on their behalf, facilitating their recovery at home. As Vijay explains it: "When we get to the point where patients have no choice but to google 'What's the best device for X condition?' we as healthcare providers have failed. We're burdening the patient, not empowering them."

Sharing Data

Shifting care from occurring in one physical clinic or hospital to the home and across multiple providers requires a greater investment in data sharing. When I worked at a large academic medical center, I often found the greatest benefit for my patients who had multiple doctors wasn't so much the doctors themselves; it was the fact that we were all on the same electronic health record system and could email or call each other when needed.

Home-based services need to achieve this level of communication—either by providing these services through one system that extends across the hospital, clinic, and home or by seamlessly coordinating between different entities—a topic I discuss in greater detail in Chapter 4.

Designing for the Needs of Vulnerable Health Populations

In many respects, bringing care into the home has enormous potential to improve access to care for our most vulnerable patients—including the elderly, individuals with disabilities, individuals living in poverty, rural communities, and racial and ethnic minorities. But this won't happen automatically. Many of our most vulnerable patients live in unstable, crowded, or unsafe housing, which is less accessible to healthcare professionals. Many elderly individuals live alone and will not be able to coordinate home-care services on their own. There are also trust issues, particularly in communities of color that have faced decades of racism and mistreatment by the medical community. Unless we explicitly design these services to address these barriers, health disparities may worsen—not improve. For example, one solution is to train and hire health workers who live within and are part of the communities they serve, a topic we discuss more in Chapter 10.

STRATEGIC ACTIONS

Today's healthcare system is designed to deliver care in clinics, hospitals, and other high-cost facilities. However, the Covid-19 pandemic has revealed the fundamental challenges with facility-based care and accelerated the move to care at home and other less dangerous and costly sites of care. But it won't be easy. We'll need to solve the last-mile problem, manage new requirements around data connectivity and care coordination, be wary of fragmentating care, and remove barriers for vulnerable health populations.

Home-based care is technologically possible. What's needed now are changes in payment and regulation, organizational capacity, and—perhaps most important—culture. The idea that healthcare happens in a clinic or hospital is deeply ingrained in the minds of doctors and patients. Covid-19 has started to shift that mindset, but we still have far to go.

Here are some steps that all of us can take to accelerate our path to home-based care and position ourselves and our organizations to succeed.

Patients, Caregivers, and Consumers of Care

- Seek out doctors, employer programs, and health plans that strive to meet patients where they are and offer a wide range of benefits and services, including telemedicine, house calls, and home-based services.

- Decide how you prefer to see the doctor—whether in a clinic, in your home, or virtually—and find a doctor who works for your needs and preferences.

Physicians and Healthcare Professionals

- Decide how best you like to serve patients and what aligns most with your values, preferences, and needs—whether online from home, through house calls, in a clinic or hospital, or some combination thereof—and then seek out a practice that provides that kind of care.

Healthcare Delivery Systems, Including Traditional and Technology Enabled

- Create a strategy around home-based care. Decide what services make the most sense for your organization to deliver and what services to coordinate through partners.

- Reinvest dollars from fixed facilities to virtual, home, and community-based models of care.

- Invest in data sharing and interoperability so that patients, purchasers of care, and partners can effectively create a seamless care experience across facility- and home-based care.

- Partner with third-party logistics and supply chain companies to solve the last-mile problem of home-based care.

- Hire and train healthcare workers who can effectively and safely deliver care in the home.

Payers, Including Employers, Government Entities, and Health Plans

- Ensure payment equity—not necessarily payment parity—between traditional care and home-based care models across a wide range of models, including home visits, high-acuity care at home, and hospital-at-home.

- Provide quality and price transparency tools and navigation services to patients so they can make better decisions about home-based care and services.

- Consider investing in internet and device access, computer literacy, and language translation services to ensure universal access to home-care services with virtual care components.

Policymakers

- Promote multipayer arrangements with hospitals and nonincumbent providers to aggregate market demand for home-based care models.

- Establish incentives and appropriate regulatory frameworks to promote the adoption of proven alternatives to facility- and hospital-based care, including mandating cross-state and/or reciprocal licensure and fast-tracking the development of necessary billing codes, appropriate safety and quality requirements, and credentialing for both clinical and nonclinical providers.

• Remove outdated restrictions to home-based care that inhibit use or limit effectiveness, for example, policies that prohibit nonphysician providers from drawing blood samples at home and patients from receiving medications by mail.

• Create standards of quality and reporting for home-based care models.

• Incentivize or mandate medical education providers to provide physicians and other healthcare professionals exposure to and training in home-based care.

Healthcare Investors and Entrepreneurs

Invest in and build companies that address the last-mile problem through the following:

• Real-time supply-demand matching and end-to-end supply chain management.

• Aggregating data across health plans and suppliers and providing price and quality transparency on home-based services and goods to help patients and families make the right choices.

• Training, staffing, and managing home-based care workforces.

• Ensuring the safety and quality of home-based care.

• Simplifying the experience of home-based care for patients and families.

• Creating medical equipment and goods that are consumer-friendly and readily deployable in the home environment.

PART II

DIGITALLY ENABLED

n May 2020, four months into the US pandemic, my mother, a type 2 diabetes patient, decided that enough was enough. After 24 years of having diabetes and 10 years of injecting herself with insulin daily, she was tired—tired of her medications, tired of checking her blood sugar every day, and tired of living with diabetes.

I was in high school when my mom was first diagnosed. Overnight, my mother's health was no longer a given. She was the foundation of our home, and now she had a serious illness, one that I didn't understand much about other than that it would affect her for the rest of her life.

As someone born and raised in India, my mother loved rice and naan and the occasional dessert of *gulab jamun*. Like so many patients with type 2 diabetes, she largely knew what she needed to do to keep her condition under control, yet struggled to do it. Time and again, I witnessed her come home from a doctor's appointment highly motivated to lose weight and eat the right things, but by her next visit a few months later, her old habits would return.

After years of poorly controlled sugars, she was put on insulin. Every day since then (or at least on most days when she felt up to it) she would steal herself away to a quiet corner of our home, draw up a syringe of insulin, and inject herself in the abdomen. But during the pandemic, this routine had become too much for her. She wanted out.

Years earlier she had learned of the idea of "curing" diabetes from me. At the time, I was a newly minted internal medicine physician and researcher at the University of Chicago. One of my patients was an elderly African American gentleman who lived on the South Side of Chicago. He had developed type 2 diabetes as a young man and had been on insulin for years. More recently, he had gotten serious about his health. As he ate healthier and shed pounds, his blood sugar fell, and with it the number of his diabetes medications. When I took him off the last of these medications, he asked me a simple question: "Dr. Nundy, am I cured of diabetes?"

My reflexive answer was to say, "Of course not. You can't cure diabetes." But I hesitated and told him I would need to get back to him. As I walked the labyrinth of hallways that led from my clinic through the hospital to the research offices where I made my second home, his question nagged at me. I knew that type 2 diabetes wasn't a condition that went away, and yet somehow his seemed to have.

Reviewing the latest research online, I found an article published a year earlier about this very question. The advent of gastric-bypass surgery had enabled some type 2 diabetes patients who had undergone the weight-loss procedure to get off all of their medications.[1] A small group of experts had convened to define this state and choose a name for it, ultimately deciding to borrow from the field of cancer: diabetes *remission*. Patients with type 2 diabetes were in remission if they maintained a normal blood sugar without the aid of diabetes medications for at least one year.[2]

My patient hadn't had weight-loss surgery, but he seemed to otherwise fit the criteria. My next question was: How often did remission from type 2 diabetes occur naturally? To answer it, I partnered with a team of researchers at Kaiser Permanente, which had one of the largest data sets in the world of patients with type 2 diabetes. When I initially proposed the study, they were incredulous. They had been studying their data for years and had never noticed any patients in remission. But they were intrigued enough to try. After a year's worth of data cleaning, false starts, and iterative testing, we came to a conclusion: remission or cure from type 2 diabetes was rare but possible.[3] My patient was right.

When I told my mother that achieving remission was possible, she became interested in the idea but wasn't sure where to get started. A year or two later, I told her about a startup company named Virta, which had created a program to help patients with type 2 diabetes do just that. The program, which they called diabetes reversal, was based on years of research showing that a ketogenic diet—a diet so limited in carbohydrate intake that the body burns fat instead of carbohydrates—could help 60 percent of patients with type 2 diabetes get off insulin and nearly all of their medications.[4]

The problem was that the treatment was very complex to administer. Often, patients needed a lot of support from nutritional experts to follow the ketogenic diet, as well as medical supervision to carefully decrease their medications so their blood sugar wouldn't get too high or too low. Most doctors didn't know about type 2 diabetes reversal, and the few who did didn't have the staff or systems in place to properly manage it. Virta had solved these challenges and now had a growing cohort of patients who had successfully reversed their diabetes.[5]

The Virta program still required a major commitment—one that my mother wasn't quite ready to take on. But in the middle of the pandemic, with nearly daily news reports about how Covid-19 was worse in patients with diabetes, my mom was finally ready to move forward.

She went to the Virta website and signed up for the service, agreeing to pay for it out of pocket. Soon she was on the phone with a Virta representative and uploading her medical records to the site. She was instructed to tell her doctor's office that she was enrolling in the program. "They were very happy because they had been taking care of me for years, and they knew that my sugar was not controlled at all," she said. She then downloaded the Virta app and was given a series of videos to watch to learn about the diet, how the program worked, and what to expect.

Soon after, my mom met her Virta doctor, Dr. Jeff Stanley, via videoconference using the app. He helped answer her final questions and approved her to begin the program. A few days later, my mother received a bright blue box in the mail welcoming her to the program. In it, nicely packaged, were a wireless scale, a wireless glucometer, an instrument for measuring her ketones, and a recipe book. She could use the app to log her glucose and ketone measurements and what she had eaten. It also enabled her to connect with other patients in the program who were dealing with many of the same questions and struggles, and to message a health coach who understood the ins and outs of the diabetes reversal program and could get in touch with Dr. Stanley whenever necessary.

The program was tough. The diet upended her life and for the first several days left her with bad headaches and fatigue. She had a lot of questions early on and texted her coach multiple times a day. Then her team introduced her to a fellow Virta member in Chicago, who like my mother was from India and a vegetarian. He shared a number of recipes and tips about maintaining a ketogenic diet with Indian vegetarian foods, which were a lifesaver for her.

Her progress was encouraging. Within three days of starting the program, Dr. Stanley messaged her to decrease her insulin dose. After over 10 years of being on insulin and only experiencing dose increases, she went from 25 units a day to 10 units, a dramatic reduction. Within weeks, she was off insulin completely. And months later, she still is.

My mom's story illustrates the promise of digitally enabled care. Her care itself isn't digital. There's no robot, no AI. She has a doctor and a health coach, even though she's never met either one in person. Instead, she sees them virtually from the comfort of her own home.

But that's not what I mean by digitally enabled. She could just as easily see Dr. Stanley and her health coach in person in a clinic from time to time, and her program would still be digitally enabled, because digital technology is making a difference to her care in a host of additional ways:

First, my mother is *connected* to her doctor and her care team in ways that she never was before. That connection is not just about the data that is sent wirelessly to them. It's also about the personal connection she has with them—a connection strengthened by her ability to communicate with them whenever she needs to.

Second, her care is *continuous*. Between visits, she is sending data daily on her weight, blood sugar, ketones, and progress adhering to the diet. This data helps reinforce the relationship she has with her care team and shortens the feedback loop between them so her care is more proactive.

Third, her care is *collaborative*. She benefits from having access to a care team, including a doctor, a coach, and peers, who work together to address her needs. She also benefits from having her family and informal caregivers brought into the process. A few weeks into the program, when I wanted to know how my mother was doing, Dr. Stanley welcomed the opportunity to set up an appointment with me as well, during which I was able to share my concerns that my mother wasn't eating enough and receive his counsel on how I could help support her.

Fourth, her care is *personalized*. The reversal team understood her preference for Indian food and a vegetarian diet from the get-go. They also continued to tailor the service to her ongoing needs. Weeks into the program, when my mom flew cross-country to Seattle to be present for the birth of her granddaughter, they adjusted their recommendations to account for the few days it would take for her to get settled into a new routine.

Fifth, her care is *responsive* to the latest scientific evidence and expert guidelines. My mom was able to get access to a cutting-edge service based on science that most doctors aren't even aware of. And it's a service that has clinical pathways built in to ensure that her care is safe and effective.

In the chapters that follow, I talk about how the future of healthcare is *digitally enabled*. Each chapter will explore a different theme that my mom's story illustrates—connected, continuous, collaborative, personalized, and responsive. The primary thread woven through all of these chapters is that digitally enabled care uses data and technology to strengthen the trusting, caring relationships that are central to healthcare.

Months into the program, my mother remains off insulin but still hasn't figured it all out. There are days when her sugars are a little high and days when she struggles with her diet. But when I recently asked my mom whether she's glad she joined the program, her response was: "*Beta*, I'm living the life I want to now and finally getting the care I need." This future is all any of us can hope for.

CHAPTER 4

CONNECTED

GIVING PATIENTS A SEAMLESS
CARE EXPERIENCE

Standing over the sink in his hotel room, a patient I'll call John sent a message that saved his life.

"I messed up. Can you call me?"

The message went to a nurse at Accolade, the healthcare company I work for.

Hundreds of miles away, the nurse, whom I'll call Colin, received the secure message sent through Accolade's mobile app and called John back. After a few minutes on the phone, the story became clear: John had tried to kill himself. He attempted to overdose on a common over-the-counter medication. And now he was scared and wanted help.

Colin was sitting in one of our offices in Arizona, feet away from our experts in mental health and substance abuse. With their support, he kept John talking. Soon John started sharing more details—the medication he took, when he had taken it, and finally, the city, hotel, and room he was in. With that last bit of information, Colin activated emergency medical services and stayed on the line with John until they arrived.

But John's initial message wasn't just a shot in the dark. It turns out that three months earlier, John had called Colin for help with open enrollment, the annual process that many of us go through to select our insurance plan and other employee benefits.

Although John's questions were fairly straightforward, and in many places would have been answered through a self-service app or automated system, Colin took the opportunity, as our frontline care teams are trained to do, to ask John how he was doing. These, what we call "fearless questions," are challenging to ask over the phone. People often just want to have their immediate questions answered and be on their way. But if you've met Colin, as I have, he's the kind of person you instantly want to get to know better and open up to.

That was fortunate for John. He shared feeling stressed out; his new job was challenging and he was also having issues on the home front. Colin engaged. He listened closely and asked questions. Ultimately, he convinced John to contact his company's employee assistance program (EAP) to access free crisis counseling and mental health services. Colin gave him the direct phone number to his EAP, then closed the call by reminding him that if he needed anything at all, he was just a call or message away.

It wasn't until three months later, when that fateful message came through, that John and Colin connected again. Fortunately, the paramedics were able to get to John in time. And after a short stay in the hospital, he was safely discharged home with a plan to follow up with a therapist.

Six months later, John sent another message: "I've hit rock bottom. I need help *today*."

Once again, Colin called right back. John's full story came out. He had been suffering from depression and alcoholism for years. It was wreaking havoc on his personal and professional life. He was ready to go into rehab, but only if Colin could get him into a facility that same day.

Colin and a small team sprang into action. They started by identifying all of the local rehab centers that were in-network—meaning covered by John's health insurance. The centers don't update their availability online, so Colin's team called them, one by one, only to find out that none of them was available to take John that same day.

They broadened their search. Eventually they found an out-of-network alcohol treatment center that could take him. Colin would find a way to get it paid for later. All John had to do now was get himself there. But there was another problem. It was an hour away by car, and after years of alcoholism, John didn't have any family or friends who were willing to drive him. The window for meeting John's goal was closing. So Colin made a decision. He called John a cab and paid for it out of his own pocket.

Six months later, John remains sober.

VISION OF CONNECTED CARE

This chapter is about the shift to connected care. When people in the healthcare industry talk about connected care, they are usually talking about technology: devices that measure blood pressure and sugar levels at home, wirelessly sending data to the cloud; data flowing between hospitals and doctors' offices; and patients accessing their health records anytime, anywhere. Healthcare needs all of that. But what John's story makes clear is why our definition of *connected care* needs to extend beyond technology to include a connection to a human being—an empathetic, caring professional whom patients trust and can easily reach when the need arises.

You don't have to look far to know that healthcare today is far from connected on either front. On the data side, healthcare lives in silos. Doctors don't talk to other doctors, clinics don't talk to hospitals, employers don't talk to insurers, and patients and their loved ones are often the last to know what's going on. When I see a new patient in clinic, I often have to take a medical history from scratch, even if they have been seen at another clinic just weeks ago. I don't have access to a list of their medications and lab tests. I don't know who their employer is and what health benefits they offer. I don't know what additional support they qualify for to manage their chronic conditions.

On the human relationships side, patients increasingly don't have one person to turn to for their healthcare needs. Today one-fourth of Americans do not have a primary care physician, a number that only keeps growing.[1] Even those who have a primary care doctor often can't reach them when the need arises.[2] As care gets more distributed, this problem may only worsen. Patients may have a primary care doctor who sees them at home or online, another doctor who sees them in a clinic for urgent issues, and another doctor they go to for their heart disease or diabetes. Add to that care that is increasingly delivered through pharmacy chains, retail stores, and patient apps, and your head starts to spin.

John's story demonstrates both sides of what's needed—and also how much further we need to go. John was connected to an empathetic and caring healthcare professional who was just a message away. And that healthcare professional had access to most of the data he needed to help John.

If John had come to my clinic and needed help managing stress at his workplace, I would have had no idea who his employer was, that he had access to a free EAP, and what phone number to call to connect him to it. As a physician with an electronic health record, I have access to a lot of data, but often not the data I need most. Fortunately, Colin did, and having access to that information allowed him to refer John to his EAP.

But even with all the data Accolade had, the fragmented nature of the healthcare system meant that John's experience was not perfect. It turned out that John never called the EAP. Like so many patients with depression and substance abuse issues, he had a hard time bringing himself to get care. (When you barely feel the will to live, how are you going to muster up the strength to call a stranger and schedule yourself for medical care?) But

Accolade didn't get data back from the EAP, which would have shown that although the nurse had referred John, he hadn't made an appointment. (This is a common problem in healthcare: an estimated one-third of referrals made by a doctor are never followed up.)[3] Had Colin known that, he may have called John a week later to encourage him to follow up. Better yet, had the systems been directly connected, he could have scheduled John for an appointment with the EAP. This isn't just a matter of convenience. Had John begun receiving assistance months earlier, he might not have slid further into the depression and alcoholism that almost cost him his life.

Later in the process, when Colin was trying to find John a rehab facility the same day, he knew which ones were covered by his health plan and which were not. While access to this information may seem routine, it isn't. As a physician, I don't have a simple way of knowing what medications and services are covered by my patients' health plan. My clinic sees patients with dozens of different health plans, each with its own portal and login, and none of which are connected to my electronic health record. It's not enough to have data. It has to be readily accessible.

While Colin could access a list of the facilities covered by John's insurance, it still took him hours to find out which ones were accepting new patients. Although many innovators have dreamed of building an "OpenTable" for medicine—where patients and care teams can see the availability of any doctor or clinic in the country and schedule an appointment—that dream remains far from reality.

On the people side, so much of what made John's story possible was his relationship with Colin. Colin was John's lifeline. Part of what enabled that connection was Colin himself. At Accolade, we assess every person we hire for empathy and then train them to deliver compassionate care. The other part was how easy it was for John to contact him. It was as simple as sending a message, or if John wanted to speak by phone, making a direct phone call. I shudder to think how a patient of mine in a similarly dire situation would get hold of me. He would need to look up our clinic phone number online, hold for several minutes, leave a message with an operator, wait for me to be called by the operator, and finally wait for me to call back. The situation not only makes connecting with me inconvenient and slow—and in cases like John's wastes precious, lifesaving minutes—but it also keeps patients from contacting me in the first place. I don't blame them.

Finally, and most important, what John needed wasn't only someone to hold his hand—although that was essential—he needed someone who could actually solve his dilemma. Colin is a registered nurse with over 15 years of clinical experience. While Colin was not providing medical care to John, his expertise and access to key information about John empowered him to triage his health needs, facilitate an admission to a rehab facility, and start an appeal with John's insurance company to get the facility covered. Every bit as important as John's connection to Colin was Colin's connection to the rest of the healthcare system.

John's story shows that we have much further to go in creating a healthcare system that's not only connected in a digital sense but also in a human sense. No amount of seamless data integration would have gotten John to confide to Colin that he was suffering from alcoholism. He didn't reveal that information until he felt comfortable and safe sharing something that very few people in his life were aware of. This is the sacred trust that healthcare professionals have with patients—the ultimate connection.

REALIZING THE VISION

Making stories of connected care like John's the norm and not the exception will take a number of changes in healthcare.

Sharing Data

About a year ago I saw the type of patient that doctors usually dread. Mrs. Rodriguez, as I'll call her, was 10 minutes late for a

15-minute appointment. As soon as I walked into the room, I knew something was very wrong. Despite her being in her early 40s, she moved to the examining table slowly and was bloated and swollen. I asked what had brought her to the clinic, and she said she recently left the hospital and needed a new doctor. I asked her why she was hospitalized, but she couldn't remember. When I noticed a surgical scar near her Adam's apple, she took out her phone to show me a series of photographs. They showed her on a ventilator with breathing tubes and catheters splayed around her. Then I asked if there was a doctor or family member I could call to find out more, but she couldn't think of anyone. She knew the name of the hospital, but I knew it would take my nurse a few hours to call and fax various request forms to track down her records. In the meantime, I had a waiting room full of patients to see.

Then my nurse made a suggestion. "Have you checked CRISP yet?" CRISP stands for Chesapeake Regional Information System for our Patients. It is a health information exchange (HIE).

Within a minute, we had Mrs. Rodriguez's full record pulled up. I instantly had access to hundreds of documents, imaging reports, and lab results. Within a couple of minutes, I found her discharge summary from the hospital.

With it, I immediately knew what to do. I went back into the room and explained to Mrs. Rodriguez why she was in the hospital. I then helped her organize her medications according to her discharge instructions and scheduled the follow-up appointments she needed.

CRISP has been a huge success in my region. To illustrate why it has been transformational, David Horrocks, CRISP's CEO, told me a story about his grandmother: When her primary care doctor put her on a blood pressure medication, the full-strength dose made her dizzy, so her doctor cut her dosage to one-quarter of the original. She handled that well, and it kept her blood pressure in the right range. However, when she was hospitalized for pneumonia a couple of years later, the hospital sent her back to her retirement community with the full dose of the blood pressure medication. As a result, she had a dizzy spell and took a nasty fall.

She recovered, but a year later she was hospitalized again. Again, she was discharged with the wrong dose of her medication. This time, David's sister, a nurse practitioner, caught the error. But when she brought it to the attention of the nurses, they didn't have the authority to change the order, and it took two days to get the prescription rewritten at the right dose.

"This is the type of thing that drove John Erickson crazy," David told me. Erickson, founder of a chain of retirement and assisted living communities headquartered in Maryland, is CRISP's founder. In 2006, after seeing seniors like David's grandmother released from hospitals with the wrong medications, he brought together the region's biggest healthcare systems to discuss how they might exchange patient information. Within a couple of years, they worked with the Maryland Health Care Commission to create the state's first health information exchange.

Today hundreds of hospitals, clinics, laboratories, and imaging centers across the region are connected to CRISP, making patient records more easily accessible and available.[4] Unlike most healthcare IT, CRISP is widely used and valued by healthcare providers. ER doctors access CRISP to get a patient's history; cancer specialists like my wife use it to view imaging reports of patients who get their follow-up care closer to home. CRISP also has a prescription drug monitoring program that lets me see all the controlled medications my patients have been given, so I can ensure that they aren't taking too many opiate medications. I like to think that CRISP may have helped spare my patient, Mrs. Rodriguez, the kind of errors that affected David's grandmother.

But we have further to go. Through CRISP, I can access data from hospitals, imaging centers, and labs across the region.

The next step is to be able to access data nationally and to expand the network to nontraditional healthcare providers like community-based organizations, digital health services, and patient apps.

In addition, we also need to understand how to share data so that it is actually used. David Horrocks says a mistake that people often make is to focus only on the data: "Sometimes what we get is 20 pages of records, and doctors don't have time for that." Instead, CRISP works with a clinical committee to prioritize data based on specific use cases, so doctors get just the data they need—no more and no less.

Connecting Systems

Ordering medications for patients to pick up from any pharmacy in the country with a couple of clicks—what's called electronic prescribing, or e-prescribing—is so routine now that many doctors and patients don't even think of it as innovative. But I remember a time when it wasn't so routine.

When I started my medical residency, I couldn't believe how time-consuming the process of ordering medications for patients in the hospital was. First, I would walk over to the patient's floor and find the medical chart. Second, I would handwrite the medication in the chart. Third, I would put the order sheet on top of a stack of papers for the floor clerk to fax to the pharmacy. Fourth, I'd wait for the clerk at the pharmacy to review the medication order and enter it into their system. Fifth, I'd call the patient's nurse or drop by the patient's room to see if the medication had been filled.

By the end of my residency, that system had completely changed. I would pull up the electronic medical record, order the medication, and click "submit." Then I would see when the medications were scheduled and be able to track in near real time when the patient received it.

But even then, when it came time to discharge a patient home, I couldn't e-prescribe the medications. I would order the medications in the electronic health record but still need to print out the prescription for the patient to take to their pharmacy. This wasn't just cumbersome. It impacted patient care. The extra step meant that sometimes patients didn't get their medications in time. By the time patients got to the pharmacy, it was often too late for them to fill it. At times, this meant patients would go one or two days without a critical medication and would wind up back in the hospital because of it.

E-prescribing is a reminder of what's possible. Today, lack of connected systems means that I can't automatically schedule my patients for a specialist visit, sign my patients up for transportation and social service programs, or enroll my patients in clinical programs offered by their employers. When I ask why, I'm often told "that's impossible" or "that's really hard" or "that's complicated." But that's not good enough. That I can order nearly any prescription medication from any pharmacy in the country in seconds is a powerful illustration of the future of connected care that we need and should demand.

Creating Seamless Care Transitions

Ultimately what patients want is a seamless experience as they go from one healthcare provider to another. What patients dread more than anything else is going to a doctor's office only to be asked, "So what brings you in today?"

Providing a seamless experience means integrating data into clinical workflows. At Accolade, we partnered with a leading mental health company called Ginger to provide virtual therapy and psychiatry services for our members. If the therapist noted that the patient's depression scores weren't improving, we wanted our nurses to escalate the case to the patient's primary care doctor. However, to do that, it wouldn't be enough for us to have data integration with the mental health company. The data would go into our system, and our nurses would have no idea where to find it or even to look. What we needed was to build a clinical workflow that automatically sent a task to one of our nurses if the scores didn't improve, prompting him or her to contact the primary care doctor.

Often, what's needed to make care seamless is not just data but a live conversation. As a resident in the hospital, I cared for patients whose conditions changed hourly. After an overnight shift, one of my jobs was to make sure the next doctor was prepared to take over for me. Although in theory all of the patient's health data was in the electronic health record, it wasn't enough. Data is retrospective. What we wanted to share was anticipatory. So between every transition from one care team to another, we'd sign out our patients one by one, telling each other what to watch out for and what to do if a patient's condition worsened.

Investing in Customer Service

In healthcare, customer service is sometimes considered a bad word. "We don't have customers, we take care of patients" is a common—and misguided—sentiment.

A lesson I learned from Accolade's advocacy service, which helped John, is that healthcare is sorely missing an obsessive focus on customer service. When I first joined the company, I kept hearing the terms "ASA" and "C-SAT." As a doctor, my mind immediately went to "aspirin"—acetylsalicylic acid or ASA for short—and as a technology geek, to satellite technology for "sat." I quickly learned what these terms meant. ASA was "average speed of answer," the amount of time it takes for a customer to reach a real live human being. C-SAT was "customer satisfaction," a measure of how people rate a service after they experience it.

Measuring these makes complete sense to me as a doctor. We cannot help patients if we don't pick up the phone. We cannot build a longitudinal relationship with someone if we don't treat people the way they expect to be treated.

Medicine has long given short shrift to the human side of care. Physicians are recruited for high exam scores and then are largely trained on the biomedical elements of care. Once we are in practice, we peer-review each other's cases based on what we write in the electronic medical record, not on how we treat patients in the exam room. To course correct, we need to hire empathetic, caring people and train them to deliver excellent service. We also need to create a supportive work environment that measures compassion fatigue and burnout and is structurally designed to prevent it.

Enabling Asynchronous Communication

The vast majority of healthcare today is synchronous—that is, the patient and doctor are communicating in real time. Visits to the doctor's office are all synchronous and most virtual visits are synchronous too. But as we move to a connected healthcare system, asynchronous communication—which doesn't require an immediate response—will become increasingly important.

There are multiple reasons for this. For one, most of us prefer text messaging and emails to phone calls. It's why my wife and I don't call each other anymore (synchronous); we text instead (asynchronous). Second, it's more efficient. A doctor can manage multiple patients at once using messaging, whereas in a live conversation or visit, they can generally help only one patient at a time. Third, and perhaps most important, asynchronous communication—like "How's that new medication going?", "Don't forget to fast before your lab tests tomorrow," and "Give me a call if your symptoms don't improve"—enables lighter-touch, more frequent communications that keep patients and doctors more connected.

It was a message after all that saved John's life.

STRATEGIC ACTIONS

The shift to connected care will leverage data and technology to create a more seamless care experience and strengthen the human relationships that are central to care. However, it will also create new demands on healthcare organizations and new risks. Increased data sharing will require new approaches for managing data security and privacy. More frequent communication between patients and care teams will require new staffing models to avoid overburdening providers. Making care more seamless will require investments in end user design and clinical workflow integration.

Here are steps that all of us can take to accelerate our path to connected care while mitigating these risks.

Patients, Caregivers, and Consumers of Care

- Find out if the organization where you work, get care, or receive health insurance offers a care navigator or advocate program like John's. Many of us have access to one but just don't know it.

- Ask your doctor to share your medical information with any doctor or organization they refer you to.

- Request a copy of your records at the end of each visit, and be sure to have it handy for your next appointment.

Physicians and Healthcare Professionals

- Give your patients a business card with your clinic's phone number and contact information on it, including after-hours coverage. Better yet, ask them to type it into their mobile phone before they leave the visit. Your patients should know at all times who to reach and how to reach them when a health concern arises.

Healthcare Delivery Systems, Including Traditional and Technology Enabled

- Create a single place that patients can call or message with any health concern or question 24/7 and measure and report your abandonment rate, wait times, and patient satisfaction.

- Make care transitions more seamless by creating standardized clinical workflows for common health conditions and referrals.

- Hire, train, and promote frontline care teams as much for compassion and empathy as for technical expertise. Build an environment that minimizes compassion fatigue. Measure and track provider and staff burnout.

- Incorporate measures of messaging, email, and asynchronous communication into metrics of provider productivity.

- Make data sharing and security—including hiring a chief data officer, a chief security officer, or other roles with clear accountability and responsibility for data and security—a strategic differentiator and a core competency for your organization.

Payers, Including Employers, Government Entities, and Health Plans

- Demand that providers, technology-enabled services, and partners invest in data interoperability and sharing.

- Invest in advocacy and care navigation services to coordinate and streamline care. Provide tools and data to empower those services to most effectively serve your members.

- Provide reimbursement for messaging, email, and asynchronous communication, or accelerate adoption of risk-based payment models that pay healthcare providers for results, not visits.

Policymakers

- Set aggressive timelines for data interoperability and sharing by making it a requirement for receiving government grants, contracts, and payments.

- Strengthen investment in health information exchanges. Data sharing is a public good.

- Reexamine patient privacy and security laws—the "portability" in the Health Insurance Portability and Accountability Act (HIPAA)—to remove unnecessary barriers to data sharing.

Healthcare Investors and Entrepreneurs

Invest in and build technology companies that:

- Power modern data exchange.

- Aggregate data from disparate sources.

- Clean, process, and structure data.

- Improve data security and privacy and enable advanced permissioning.

- Enable physicians and other healthcare professionals to manage multiple communication channels through automation and task shifting.

- Layer care advocacy and other human-powered healthcare services on top of self-service tools.

CHAPTER 5

CONTINUOUS

MONITORING AND SUPPORTING
BEHAVIOR CHANGE EACH DAY

Many of my ideas about digitally enabled care come from a series of experiments I ran as a newly graduated primary care physician on the South Side of Chicago. I was dismayed by the large number of patients whose diabetes or heart failure took them in and out of the hospital, even though we had the medications and the science to manage them effectively.

My assessment of the problem was straightforward: patients often forget to take their medications and change their diet and physical activity. So I designed a simple solution to provide them with daily reminders delivered to their cell phone. Drawing on a past life as an MIT engineer, I developed a rudimentary software program that sent patients automated text messages about their medications and self-care. Then I designed a pilot study and enrolled a handful of patients with type 2 diabetes to receive the reminders each day for one month.

To my delight, the pilot was an overwhelming success. Patients' adherence with their medications jumped from 73 to 91 percent.[1] What's more, the benefits persisted after the reminders stopped, suggesting that patients formed new habits. "Not bad for a software program that took a few days to write and that could be rolled out at virtually no cost," I thought.

But the senior physician-researchers who oversaw my research—Marshall Chin and Monica Peek—whom I affectionately called "Dad" and "Mom," weren't as impressed. "Dad," who was well known for answering questions from his junior researchers with homemade parables, simply said, "Ask them why it worked," before ushering me out of the room to figure out next steps with "Mom."

Six months later, I tucked into my home office, ready for a long, boring night. I had 18 hour-long audio recordings to listen to. They were from in-depth interviews with the pilot participants in which they were asked about the effects of the text message reminders on their diabetes. I already knew what they would say—or so I thought. Within minutes, I realized how wrong I was:

"I was checking my text messages because I knew Marla was watching."

"I kept responding to the messages, 'cause you know, Marla would catch that."

"I didn't want to let Marla down."

Marla?

Then it dawned on me. Marla Solomon was the research coordinator who enrolled the patients in the study. As with all research studies, patients needed to give their informed consent to participate. And that role fell to Marla.

Marla is an energetic, warm, and deeply empathetic woman who had spent over 30 years advocating and caring for individuals with diabetes. A licensed diabetes educator, she had served dozens of roles within our university on various research studies and grants and in leadership roles across the state on diabetes awareness and education.

On paper, Marla's role was simply to enroll patients in the study and then monitor their text messages for safety reasons. But knowing Marla, I wasn't surprised to learn that patients had built a deep connection with her and saw her as the person behind the messages—even though they were told the messages were automated.

What made the program effective, I realized, was the combination of the daily reminders and Marla herself.

Based on these findings, we conducted a larger research study, offered to hundreds of patients for six months in partnership with their health plan. This time we designed the program so that the human connection was not an accident, but actually built into the program. Here's how it worked: A registered nurse at the health plan, Arnell Bussie, enrolled the patients over the phone. The next day, they started getting daily text messages on a broad range of topics from medications to healthy eating to physical activity to stress management. Some of the messages were reminders like, "It's time to take your medications." Others would ask a question such as, "Did you take your medications today? Please reply yes or no." If a patient's responses suggested they needed extra help, Arnell would call them to find out what was going on, offer education and counseling, and if needed, reach out to their primary care doctor.[2]

We had gone from a technology that sent text messages to a new system of continuous care enabled by technology and a relationship with a caring, empathetic person.

This time our research study showed that over a six-month period, patients not only improved their medication-taking, eating, and other habits, as we had seen in the pilot study, but also had meaningfully better health. Quality of life improved compared to before the study and blood sugar levels among participants with poorly controlled diabetes dropped from an average hemoglobin A1c (a measure of blood sugar control over three months) of 10.3 percent to 8.5 percent—the equivalent of adding a new diabetes medication.[3]

Participants received multiple "touches" from the health system—on average, over three messages a day. Compare that to the status quo, in which a patient might see a doctor one day, get their test results a week later, and then not hear back from them for three to six months. The result was a significant improvement in patients' satisfaction.

The health system was also getting more touches from the patient. Patients responded to about half the questions they received, with a median response time of under 20 minutes. In effect, the health system was receiving valuable data about patients' health in close to real time.

Care was also more efficient. In typical disease-management or coaching programs, nurses will check in with every patient once a week or once every two weeks. Instead, in our program, Arnell only checked in when patients needed her, which, on average, was just once a month. This meant that one nurse could support 400 patients at a time compared to the industry norm of one nurse per 50 to 100 patients.

It also lowered costs. Our study showed savings of over $800 per patient from fewer emergency room visits and hospitalizations—net of the cost of the program itself.

Our model of continuous care had achieved the elusive "triple aim": it made patients happier and healthier, improved the experience and quality of care, and made healthcare more affordable.

VISION OF CONTINUOUS CARE

Continuous care is about delivering care when health happens—every day—rather than only when visits to the doctor happen. It's about getting data more routinely by connecting to patients and devices between visits, and then acting on that data when the need arises. Key is shifting from formal, periodic visits with a doctor to informal, frequent check-ins with a care team.

The shift to continuous care is essential for one very simple reason: today healthcare is discrete, while health is continuous. Healthcare is organized around individual events—a visit to the doctor, a surgery, a hospitalization—with little support or care in between. This episodic approach may be fine for acute issues—you break your arm and get a cast, you have appendicitis and undergo surgery, you develop pneumonia and receive antibiotics—but not for conditions that are chronic. As the population has aged, our understanding of disease has advanced and our ability to help patients survive once deadly conditions has improved, medicine has increasingly shifted to preventive and chronic care. Today we understand that our health is largely a result of the steps we take, or don't take, each day. This means that healthcare needs to be about behavioral change—behaviors that happen outside the walls of the traditional healthcare system.

The need for healthcare to extend its reach into the daily lives of patients is sometimes referred to as the "5,000 hours problem." There are 5,000 waking hours of the year. Whether or not patients control their chronic conditions depends largely on what they do during those 5,000 hours, yet they only access the healthcare system an hour or two per year. If we expect to meaningfully move the needle on preventive and chronic care, we need to deliver care more continuously.

BARRIERS TO CONTINUOUS CARE

The term *continuous care* may conjure up an image of a futuristic Apple watch—a wearable device with wireless sensors—that streams data on our blood pressure, sugar levels, and a host of other physiologic measures for doctors to evaluate in real time. That vision, while compelling, is somewhat fanciful for a number of reasons.

For one, it suffers from what I call the "double compliance" problem. The patients who need these devices the most are often the ones least likely to use them. Many of the same barriers that hinder people from adhering to many of the healthy behaviors that keep their chronic conditions in control in the first place also make it more difficult for them to adopt these devices. Having a powerful wireless device is great, but it requires patients to adopt a new lifestyle behavior (for example, using the device) in order to adopt a new health behavior (for example, running, eating healthy, taking their medications). Hence the term "double compliance."

Second, it imposes new demands on the doctor. We already have a shortage of doctors. A world in which data is continuously transmitted to doctors in real time may sound great, but for doctors, it's a massive distraction that risks overburdening them more than they already are. In fact, a recent study showed that clinicians with the highest volume of patient messages had almost four times the odds of burnout compared to clinicians with the fewest.[4] Not only is getting continuous data tedious and time consuming, but also the data isn't likely to be very useful. Most things that happen on a moment-to-moment basis do not warrant medical attention. In fact, paying attention to and acting on all of that data risks subjecting patients to more care than they need—and that can actually cause harm[5] and make care more expensive.

Third, and perhaps the most important reason why this vision is limited, is that it misses the core of medicine, which is the human relationship. Streaming data alone from the patient to the doctor is unlikely to strengthen the doctor-patient relationship. In fact, it may worsen it.

I saw this play out firsthand during my medical residency. When I started, our hospital hadn't yet implemented an electronic health record. If, in the middle of the night, I wanted to check a patient's vital signs or even order Tylenol, I had to leave my call room, walk over to the nursing station closest to the patient's room, and locate the patient's chart (sometimes the most time-consuming part!). On the way back, I'd often check in on the patient just to see how they were feeling or see if a medication had been given. Sometimes, we'd fall into a conversation that would reveal important parts of their care—their challenging living situation, a deeply held misconception about their disease, or just basic questions they had about why they were in the hospital and how they could keep from having to come back again.

After our hospital implemented an electronic health record, the way we practiced medicine fundamentally changed. We increasingly managed our patients as if operating from a remote command center. From our workroom filled from one end to the other with computers, we saw our patients' data, ordered medications, and called nurses. The fact that we were just feet away from our patients and nurses seemed to be more a nuisance than a necessity. Gone were the causal "drive-bys."

But it wasn't just the transfer of charts from the patient wards to our computers that led to this profound shift. As charts went online, our interns started getting more and more data. Everything was now computerized—every vital sign, every medication, every time a nurse changed a patient's bedsheets—all of it logged and uploaded. But it seemed to me that the more data we had about our patients, the less we knew them.

In the process, our work became a lot less fun. No more war stories from veterans we were taking care of or late-night laughter with nurses. To be sure, there was also a lot less of the painful stuff—like wasting precious time locating a patient's chart or chasing down a medication order—but the bright spots were gone too.

I'm not suggesting that we go back to the "good old days" of medicine. Before electronic health records, hospital care was less safe and more inefficient. Rather, the point is that we need to consider how we can preserve caring, empathetic relationships between patients and doctors as we move into a continuous-care world.

The way forward may lie in what I've come to think of as the "Marla experiment," the research study I discussed at the start of the chapter. For me there were three key lessons:

1. **Continuous care should build and strengthen relationships between patients and care teams.**

   What made patients engage with our system was the fact that somebody somewhere was monitoring it. That person did not need to send every message or read every reply. She just needed to be around—hovering virtually. If we reflect on our personal lives, that makes sense: How many of us have bought a fitness tracker or downloaded an exercise app only to abandon it weeks later? If no one is there to cheer us on, we give up. What sustains us is the human connection.

   Technology can also help that human caregiver know when to go from hovering to intervening. In our experiment, one of the most powerful triggers for Arnell, our nurse, to reach out to patients was when people stopped responding to the automated messages altogether. We interpreted this as a signal that the patient wasn't just disengaging with the messaging program, they could also be disengaging with their care. In one case, a patient hadn't responded to the messages because her sister was in the hospital. In her state of worry, she had stopped responding to the messages and also stopped taking her insulin. The call from Arnell, which provided her a "virtual hug" and encouragement over the phone, was all she needed to get back on track with her diabetes regimen.

2. **Continuous care should meet patients where they are.**

   We started the Marla experiment in 2010 when many of my patients, who came from a low-income community, didn't have smartphones. We purposely designed the entire system to work on text messages because that was what my patients used. Many didn't have landlines because they didn't have stable housing. Most couldn't afford a smartphone or high-speed internet, so they had a basic cellphone. They didn't make phone calls because texts were free and calls were expensive. So we piggybacked our continuous care model on a technology that our patients were already using to avoid the double compliance issue I discussed earlier.

Using basic cellphones also made our program more inclusive. Whenever I see a fancy new gadget for improving health, my first concern is how my least well-off patients will get access to it. Instead of introducing a new technology, we should ask ourselves how we can leverage the technology patients already have and use to accomplish the same ends.

3. Continuous care should be integrated within the overall healthcare system.

What we ultimately built was not a series of texts or even a text messaging or mobile health program. What we built was a new system of care that was integrated into the healthcare system.

Patients didn't interact with just any nurse. They were supported by a nurse from their health plan. Moreover, this nurse could contact patients' primary care doctors when needed. As a result, patients were continuously connected to someone who not only had the clinical expertise to provide them education and coaching but also could help them get the medical care they needed. When a patient wasn't taking their medication because it cost too much, the nurse knew what other medications were better covered by their insurance. She even had it in her power to waive the co-pays. She could also reach out to the patient's doctor for assistance. In short, the program worked because it leveraged the existing system, rather than operating outside of it.

Creating this system required integrating it into each stakeholder's clinical workflow. For patients, who were already managing their diabetes and using their phones every day, their phones were now helping them manage their diabetes. For the nurse, who already called patients with claims or health issues, the messaging software was now sending her action items that she added to her daily task list. For physicians, who were already accustomed to receiving emails and phone calls from nurses, the program appeared to be business as usual. It didn't require them to enroll patients in a messaging system or log onto a different software system to review the alerts.

The need to integrate the program into existing workflows was explicitly why we didn't ask patients to message us their blood sugars—something that I was asked time and again when I presented the results of our model nationally. Sometimes patients' blood sugars can be dangerously high or low, a situation that requires immediate attention. But neither the nurse's daily task list nor email notifications to the doctor were appropriate for this. So rather than force fit a model that wouldn't work, we designed around the existing one.

COMPONENTS OF CONTINUOUS CARE

As the Marla experiment showed, a handful of things are required to make continuous care successful. We need a way to know what's going on with patients when they are not in the health system. That is, we need data, ideally daily. In our experiment, the data were the text replies we received. We also need a way to know which patients need additional help. In the experiment, we built a set of simple rules to determine when to alert the nurse.

Finally, we need to change patients' behavior. In our experiment, we used text messages designed to establish new habits around medication taking, healthy eating, physical activity, and monitoring their conditions.

The Marla experiment was quite crude. The following are examples of more sophisticated approaches to each of these components.

Getting Data from Patients: Remote Monitoring

Remote monitoring, systems that use connected devices to collect data from patients and transmit it to medical professionals, has been used in a wide range of conditions from diabetes (monitoring blood sugars) to Parkinson's disease (monitoring gait) to Covid-19 (monitoring oxygen levels).

The classic use case is heart failure. Patients with heart failure have to watch their fluid and salt intake on a daily basis. Simple home measurements like weight and blood pressure can detect early signs of impending heart failure. But if a patient forgets to check these measurements—or they find their weight and blood pressure creeping up but don't call their doctor—they can wind up in the hospital, ICU, or worse.

Giving these patients a wireless blood pressure monitor and scale to transmit these data to a doctor seems like an obvious solution. However, research studies of remote monitoring in heart failure show that it doesn't always make a difference. To find out why, I called my colleague Joe Kvedar, a physician at Mass General Brigham and an expert in digital health.

Joe pointed me to a study conducted by researchers at Yale in 2010. The Yale team had been buoyed by the results of an earlier study of remote monitoring in heart failure that enrolled 88 patients who had just been released from the hospital. Half the patients were counseled in person by an exceptionally dedicated cardiac nurse (another Marla), who then followed up with regular phone calls over the next year to ask them about their weight and other symptoms. The other half received the usual care from their doctor. At the end of the year, the group who had regular chats with the nurse had 39 percent fewer hospitalizations than the control group.[6]

But that study was confined to the Yale–New Haven medical center. When the team decided to run a larger study at several locations, they knew it would be too expensive to have a nurse at each site. Instead, patients in the treatment group were asked to call an automated system each day to report their weight and symptoms. There was no nurse interaction unless the parameters suggested a need for a call from a doctor. Six months later the researchers found that both groups had similar rates of hospitalization and death. Their conclusion: "Telemonitoring did not improve outcomes." However, one important point was lost in the summary—almost half of the patients in the telemonitoring group failed to use the phone system as instructed. By the end of the study, only 55 percent were calling in their data even three times a week, and 14 percent never made a single call.[7]

As Joe sees it, two factors contributed to the study's dismal results. "It was extra work for the patients. And because there was no human connectivity, it was a miserable failure." That "extra work" is a barrier he's come up against before. He told me about a small study his team conducted using two different devices to transmit blood pressure readings. One device required patients to take their blood pressure and then push a button to transmit their reading. The other device automatically sent the data after the patients took their blood pressure—no push required. Thirty days later, Joe's team found that the first group had entered only a third as many readings as the second.[8] "The simple requirement to do one small thing threw off adherence," he said.

Making Sense of the Data: Artificial Intelligence

As healthcare gets more connected and there is more and more data to sift through, simple rules-based logic like the one we created for the Marla experiment will no longer be sufficient. What we need are more sophisticated tools to separate the signal from the noise. This is key if we hope to get doctors just the alerts they need without causing alert fatigue from those they don't.

Artificial intelligence (AI) is one such tool, but applying it in healthcare is easier said than done, as I learned from Mark Sendak, a physician and data scientist at the Duke Institute for Health Innovation. Mark once told me about a patient with kidney disease who had undergone more that 50 tests of his kidney function over a three-year period. The tests were ordered by different doctors for different reasons. Some tests were ordered in the emergency room when the patient had an acute issue; others were ordered by outpatient doctors who helped him manage his various chronic health conditions. If you plot the patient's kidney function tests on a graph, as Mark has, you see that his kidney function tests went up and down in the short term. However, overall, they trended down from normal kidney function toward what doctors call end-stage kidney disease. Because the blood tests were done at different hospitals and bounced up and down from one visit to the next, none of his doctors caught the downward trend. By the time someone did, it was too late. He ended up on dialysis. The question he asked his physician was, "Doc, why didn't anyone tell me sooner?"

The patient's story motivated Mark and his team to come up with an answer. They decided to build a computer program that would mine the records of thousands of patients and predict which patients had declining kidney function and needed intervention. That project, which Mark thought would take a few weeks, ended up taking two years! First, he needed access to the data, which was stuck in different silos and required different permissions and steps to acquire. Then the data wasn't what data scientists call "clean." Because the health system had changed the test it used to measure kidney function two years earlier, Mark couldn't just combine data across years. Instead, he needed to spend hundreds of hours manipulating the data into a common standard. Finally, he and his team built and validated a predictive model using AI to accurately identify which patients were at the highest risk of serious kidney disease.[9] Although this sounds like the most complicated step, in many respects it was the easiest.

The hardest part was yet to come. He needed to convince doctors to actually use the algorithm he had created. That meant finding a way to integrate it into their workflow. After multiple fits and starts, Mark landed upon a very low-tech solution—his team organized a weekly case conference in which a primary care physician, kidney specialist, and nurse care manager gathered to review the charts of patients with the highest risk scores and discuss what to do.

That final step is key, Mark says. "Everything I've built has been human-in-the-loop. What I've learned is how important it is to have the right human in the loop at the right time and with the right information."

Changing Patient Behavior: Digital Therapeutics

The ultimate form of continuous care is for patients to manage their own conditions. Increasingly, patients are using smartphone apps for that purpose—from tracking nutrition and exercise to recording their blood sugars to meditating and reducing stress. In many respects, the Marla study was a "patient app," even though it technically wasn't on a smartphone.

Although the app store offers hundreds of thousands of healthcare apps,[10] very few have been proven to improve health outcomes. Moreover, long-term engagement, particularly among patients who need them most, is often poor. It is clear that digital technologies will be essential in the shift to continuous care. However, to deliver on their promise, they need to be designed to create sustained behavior change and be proven to engage and improve the health of a diverse set of patients.

Enter digital therapeutics. Digital therapeutics are digital technologies that deliver evidence-based therapeutic interventions to prevent, manage, or treat a medical disorder or disease. What makes digital therapeutics distinct from other health apps is that they have proven therapeutic value. Like new drugs for diabetes or cancer, they are often evaluated in randomized controlled studies and sometimes undergo FDA approval. For example, Blue Star, a digital assistant for people with diabetes, conducted a randomized controlled study that found significant improvements in blood glucose levels when patients used Blue Star for 12 months.[11]

While the field is still in its infancy, digital therapeutics exist today for a wide range of conditions across prevention, chronic diseases, and mental health. QuitGenius is a digital behavioral change program that helps patients stop smoking. Omada Health and Blue Mesa Health help patients prevent type 2 diabetes and manage chronic conditions by promoting healthy habits and closely monitoring patient activity levels, diet, and weight. In mental health, Happify is a digital therapeutic for depression and anxiety and Freespira is designed for panic attacks and post-traumatic stress disorders.

WHAT WE NEED TO MAKE
CARE MORE CONTINUOUS

Despite the fact that the Marla experiment was a home run—it made patients happier and healthier and lowered healthcare costs—a decade later, programs like it remain the exception and not the rule. To realize the vision of continuous care, the system will need to be transformed in a number of ways.

Changes in the Way We Pay for Care

Care today is organized around in-person visits in large part because payment is organized around in-person visits. In recent years, new payment codes for remote monitoring and other continuous care modalities have been developed. However, ultimately, the greater shift will happen when we move to risk-based capitated payment models, in which healthcare providers receive a fixed amount of money to care for patients and then can decide on their own how best to care for them—a topic I consider in greater depth in Chapter 9.

New Technologies for Healthcare Providers

Because electronic health records are designed around billing and coding, they, too, are organized around discrete patient visits. Today, my electronic health record shows me a list of my patient appointments for the day. In a continuous care world, my day might instead be organized around tasks—some of which will be patient appointments, but many of which will be follow-up actions I need to take or alerts I need to respond to. In addition, I should be able to access a health dashboard of all of my patients prioritized according to who needs the most attention. This would allow me to best use my time each day to optimize the health of my entire patient population.

New Technologies for Patients

Patients will need technology, too. The ideal is to use tools that patients already have like we did in the Marla experiment, but this won't always be feasible or desirable. In my mom's diabetes reversal story, the wireless glucose monitor and scale were provided to her as part of the program. However, my mom was expected to have her own smartphone and high-speed connectivity. Greater investments will be needed for those on the other side of the digital divide—including individuals living in poverty, the elderly, racial and ethnic minorities, and rural communities—to ensure that these programs don't leave patients behind and worsen health disparities. For example, in 2016 when the

Department of Veterans Affairs implemented a telehealth program in remote areas, they distributed video-enabled tablets to over 6,000 patients to bridge the digital divide.[12]

Investments in Data

We need to be able to receive, clean, store, share, and interpret healthcare data, so that the work of experts like Mark Sendak is easier. Moreover, we need to expand beyond traditional biomedical data—for example, data on social determinants of health (e.g., housing, food security) and patient-reported outcomes (e.g., quality of life, functional status). As we get more and more data, it will become increasingly difficult for doctors to separate the signal from the noise and to avoid being overburdened by data. Artificial intelligence holds great promise, but needs to be designed to be understandable by humans—doctors and other healthcare professionals—who ultimately need to use the information to help patients.

New Regulations

We need to make it simple for patients to collect their own data and communicate with their physicians and care teams between visits, ideally with tools that they already own and use routinely. Using text messaging may require relaxing restrictions that are designed to protect patient privacy and security. Despite its positive impact on diabetes and costs, the Marla experiment never got past the research stage—in part because of concerns from hospital administrators that text messaging did not comply with HIPAA privacy and security regulations. During Covid-19, we saw how relaxing some of these restrictions improved access without compromising patient security.[13] In my clinic, which serves a low-income, largely Spanish-speaking community, the ability to use FaceTime and WhatsApp, which are not considered HIPAA secure, made the difference between seeing a doctor or not.

A Focus on Healthcare Relationships

We need to hire healthcare workers like Marla on the other end of continuous care systems, and then train and support them in the right work environments and culture. We also need to direct alerts to the same healthcare worker when possible—to enable them to build longitudinal, trusting relationships with patients.

The key to continuous care can be most aptly summed up in this quote from one of the patients in the Marla study: "Just knowing that somebody somewhere cared and was watching—that's what made the difference."

STRATEGIC ACTIONS

The shift to continuous care will create new opportunities to drive behavior change, thus improving patient outcomes and lowering healthcare costs, but only if these systems are designed to strengthen relationships between patients and their care teams and to integrate into clinical workflows.

Here are some steps that all of us can take to accelerate our path to continuous care and position ourselves and our organizations to succeed.

Patients, Caregivers, and Consumers of Care

* Seek out doctors and services that integrate remote monitoring, patient apps, and other forms of continuous care, especially if you have a condition for which these care models are proven to improve outcomes, such as obesity, smoking, mental health issues, type 2 diabetes, high blood pressure, and heart failure.

- Find out if your employer or health insurance company offers disease management or coaching programs that use connected devices or self-tracking apps.

- If you own a fitness tracker or wearable device, print out or email a one-page screenshot of your data to share with your primary care doctor at your next routine visit.

Physicians and Healthcare Professionals

- Create a "formulary" of evidence-based patient apps and self-service tools and "prescribe" them to your patients as part of your routine care. For example, I often recommend free mindfulness apps to my patients.

Healthcare Delivery Systems, Including Traditional and Technology Enabled

- Seek out new payment models that enable you to begin the transformation to continuous care, such as remote patient monitoring, or accelerate your transition to risk-based payment models.

- Invest in system transformation and quality improvement when implementing a continuous care model to ensure that it improves quality and outcomes.

- Choose technology partners that integrate into the electronic health record, and invest in as much technology and clinical integration as is required until doctors are consistently using them in routine clinical practice.

- Carefully consider provider-patient communication policies to balance meeting patients where they are with privacy and security concerns.

- Hire, train, and support healthcare workers who are empathetic and caring and able to build trusting relationships digitally.

Payers, Including Employers, Government Entities, and Health Plans

- Shift to value-based care models, including global capitation and bundled payments that will spur investment and innovation in continuous care models that are aligned with value.

- Invest in remote monitoring, patient apps, and other continuous care services that are proven to improve health outcomes, and then measure their performance in your patient population.

Policymakers

- Provide clear regulatory guidance on technologies that support continuous care to ensure safety and efficacy while encouraging investment and innovation.

- Invest in internet connectivity and hardware for communities affected by the digital divide.

- Create a market for continuous care technologies that are designed to meet the unique needs of racial and ethnic minorities and other vulnerable health populations through multistakeholder calls for proposals.

Healthcare Investors and Entrepreneurs

Invest in and build companies that enable continuous care by:

- Leveraging social support and other behavioral science approaches to optimize engagement.

- Building and strengthening human relationships with physicians and other traditional and nontraditional healthcare professionals.

- Integrating within clinical workflows without overburdening providers.

- Enabling management by exception through the use of remote monitoring and reducing alert fatigue by using AI and continual learning.

- Rigorously and independently measuring and tracking clinical outcomes.

- Building for the needs of individuals living in poverty, the elderly, rural communities, and racial and ethnic minorities.

CHAPTER 6

COLLABORATIVE

BRINGING MULTIPLE DOCTORS, CAREGIVERS, AND PEERS TOGETHER

Weeks into medical school, I saw a patient who forever shaped my perspective on the need for collaboration in healthcare. As first-year medical students, my classmates and I had been spending most of our time in the classroom learning anatomy, biochemistry, and physiology. The highlight was when we got to learn "clinical skills," the basics of taking a patient history and conducting a physical exam. After weeks of practice on each other, we finally had the opportunity to try our hands (quite literally) on real patients.

As usually happens, our course administrators found us the nicest patients in the hospital to practice on—patients who understood that we might ask too many questions and strike our reflex hammers a little too hard, yet still agreed to let us learn from them.

I got the opportunity to meet Ms. Sarah, as I'll call her, a 26-year-old woman who was stationed on a military base in

Southeast Asia when she began experiencing nightly fevers. At first, she thought she had a simple cold that would go away on its own. When her symptoms persisted for several days, she decided to see a doctor. Being stationed in Southeast Asia, she was tested for a wide range of tropical diseases common to that part of the world. The tests came back negative, but the fevers persisted, so her doctors gave her a course of antibiotics just to see if that would help. It didn't.

She quickly became a medical mystery, traveling first to Okinawa, then to Germany, then to Walter Reed National Military Medical Center, and finally to Johns Hopkins where I was a student. Over the course of a few months, she saw dozens of doctors and had hundreds of tests performed. Sometimes the tests would turn out mildly positive, sending the doctors on a wild goose chase, and other times the fevers would subside for a day, only to come back again.

The day I met her, she was about to be discharged from Johns Hopkins Hospital—often the final resort for patients with medical problems that can't be solved anywhere else—yet again without a diagnosis. Despite her ordeal, she was extraordinarily kind and generous, as patients so often are, humoring my too many questions and, yes, my clumsy and overeager, reflex hammer.

Just as I was wrapping up our session, an elderly physician barged in. After asking a series of questions and examining her skin and reflexes (much more expertly than I had, I noted), he announced, "I know exactly what this is, and you'll be better in no time," before marching out of the room. I later learned he was a retired infectious disease doctor—one of the legends of Johns Hopkins. In the chart hanging on her hospital door, he left a handwritten note explaining the diagnosis and recommending a course of high-dose ibuprofen. Within days, Ms. Sarah was feeling better, and within weeks she was back to serving our country.

I've thought about Ms. Sarah many times over the years. Somebody somewhere knew exactly what she had, and yet she had suffered for months, seen dozens of doctors, and racked up tens of thousands of dollars in medical bills and travel costs. Even then, it was almost by sheer luck that she was finally diagnosed and treated. I began thinking that there ought to be a way for patients like her to more easily access the expertise of not just one but multiple doctors.

This was the first—but not the last—time during my training that I saw an opportunity for greater collaboration in medicine. As I rotated through the hospital and clinics, I saw that it wasn't just patients like Ms. Sarah with unsolvable mysteries who benefited from greater levels of expertise. As a resident on the hospital wards, I'd go on rounds with teams of doctors, who often shared the same specialty but brought widely different experiences and perspectives to our patients. It wasn't necessarily the most senior physicians who knew all the answers. I still remember a medical student—fresh from her exams and textbooks—who suggested that a patient might have a very rare presentation of lupus. We humored her by ordering a battery of diagnostic tests, only to find that she was right.

The benefits of collaborating on rounds extended beyond diagnosis. How often was it that a member of the team picked up on a key detail that the rest of us had missed—like the fact that the patient wasn't actually taking their insulin or didn't have a stable home to go back to? And how often had our discussions on rounds allowed us to come up with better answers—like how exactly would repeating that MRI change our management? The primary purpose of rounding was teaching and education, but it was also a form of collaborative care.

Later, when I got an MBA to better understand service delivery models in healthcare and other industries, I started seeing the benefits of collaboration elsewhere in medicine. When we read a Harvard Business School case study on the Spine Center at Dartmouth–Hitchcock Medical Center, I saw how a key aspect of their model was that patients with back pain could see multiple specialists at once—back surgeons, neurologists, physical therapists, and mental health professionals—not only for their convenience but also to enable a team of doctors to make decisions at one time together.[1] I saw similar kinds of collaboration in my wife's training as a cancer doctor through the tumor board—a weekly case conference where medical oncologists, surgical oncologists, and radiation oncologists come together to make decisions about surgery, chemotherapy, and radiation.

During my fellowship in health services research, I also studied the benefits of collaboration beyond physicians in models of team-based care that included doctors, nurses, pharmacists, and other healthcare professionals and in peer support models like Alcoholics Anonymous (AA). I learned about its application to depression and anxiety in the work of researchers at the University of Washington who developed a model of care designed to integrate mental health back into physical health called IMPACT—otherwise known as the collaborative care model. In an early study, individuals with diabetes and depression had a 70 percent improvement in their depression symptoms and a 30 percent improvement in their diabetes outcomes. The model lowered unnecessary hospitalizations and had an impressive six-to-one return on investment, meaning for every dollar spent on the program, it saved the healthcare system six dollars.[2]

The benefits of collaboration seemed to be everywhere. And yet, when I finally got out of training into the real world of medicine, I saw that, except in academic medical centers and certain specialized fields of medicine, collaboration was largely absent in practice.

VISION OF COLLABORATIVE CARE

This chapter will explore *collaborative care*, which I define as care that involves multiple healthcare professionals, informal caregivers, and peers working together for the benefit of the patient. Collaborative care reimagines the one-to-one model of care that has defined medical practice for centuries and shifts it to a many-to-one model. No longer will care be assumed to happen between one doctor and one patient. Instead, we will acknowledge that patients have and need many caregivers—multiple doctors and other types of healthcare professionals, loved ones and informal caregivers, and peers—and that healthcare needs to be designed to enable greater collaboration among them.

Imagine if Ms. Sarah's care had been more collaborative. She goes to see her doctor for fevers. He orders some tests, but they came back inconclusive and he isn't sure what to do next. With a click of a button, her doctor sends her case information to a specialist who, within a day, reviews her information and weighs in on what to do. Her case doesn't go to just any specialist. Instead, it's routed to the most expert doctor based on the specifics of her case—including her medical history, laboratory tests, and possible diagnosis.

In some cases, that expert is able to help guide the doctor and the patient on the best course of action without having to see the patient. But in this case, he needs to take a history directly from Ms. Sarah. So the next day, a virtual visit is scheduled. From her base in Southeast Asia, Ms. Sarah answers the expert's questions. She also hears firsthand what he thinks is going on, which helps put her mind at ease. After the visit, the expert's recommendations are shared with Ms. Sarah's doctor. Additional tests are ordered for her to complete the next day.

From there, the case is routed to higher and higher levels of care, bringing in increasing levels of expertise as needed. In some cases, family members are invited to these video conferences because oftentimes they can provide information that helps crack a challenging case. Ms. Sarah's case is expedited to a diagnosis board at which doctors from multiple disciplines—infectious diseases, rheumatology, and mental health—review her case and consider a diagnosis. Rather than subjecting Ms. Sarah to yet another interview, they are able to access video recordings of her prior visits. They also review her lab results and medical records. Part of the aim of these multidisciplinary teams is to reduce the cognitive biases that specialists tend to have. ("When you're a hammer, everything looks like a nail.") In Ms. Sarah's case, this leads to the answer. Her fevers weren't infectious in origin; she has a rare autoimmune condition called adult onset Still's disease. That she was stationed in Southeast Asia was a red herring.

Within a week of her initial visit, Ms. Sarah is put on treatment and starts her journey to recovery. She recovers quickly and completely. If, instead, her condition were chronic, she would be directed to a patient support group where she could be comforted by other patients like her and learn from their shared experiences.

In this vision of collaborative care, Ms. Sarah isn't trekking from continent to continent in search of a diagnosis. From the comfort of her home and with her primary care physician guiding her care every step of the way, she was able to access a wide network of experts who seamlessly collaborate to provide her the best possible care.

Collaborative care embraces the reality that the average older adult sees two primary care doctors and five specialists a year,[3] and that the pace of medical innovation and progress is such that it is impossible for any one doctor to keep up to date in every field. It also acknowledges that patients often don't manage their health alone. Informal caregivers—family, friends, and peers—often play a significant and crucial role.

The result is that patients will have unprecedented access to medical expertise and support. They will no longer be limited to doctors in their geographic area. Instead, they will be able to get care from whichever doctor or institution in the country is best suited for them. In my mom's case, she got care from a startup company on the other side of the country that is specialized in reversing type 2 diabetes.

Collaborative care will permeate all facets of healthcare. When patients are transported in an ambulance, they will benefit not only from a paramedic who is able to provide lifesaving interventions but also from a virtual consultation with an emergency room doctor and if needed, a specialist. When patients are seen in clinic, they will benefit from family and friends providing context about their social needs. When patients need specialist expertise, they will access it without traveling to another doctor's office or worrying about how the information gets back to their primary care doctor.

Fortunately, many of the components of collaborative care that I describe in the hypothetical version of Ms. Sarah's case are already being incorporated into medicine. Primary care physicians are now able to virtually share a patient case with a specialist and get feedback on clinical questions—a process called an electronic consult, or e-consult. Patients are able to get a second opinion from an expert outside of their primary medical institution and are increasingly able to do so virtually. Multiple doctors are able to see a patient at one time in a multidisciplinary clinic or discuss a complex patient at a multidisciplinary case conference.

What's largely missing today is the widespread democratization of these models. What we need is to make collaborative care more routine.

CASE STUDY: THE HUMAN DIAGNOSIS PROJECT

Ms. Sarah was on my mind when nearly 10 years later a friend of mine, Jay Komarneni, approached me with a bold idea. What if we could make the world's collective medical expertise available to anyone anywhere?

Inspired by other collaborative projects like the Human Genome Project—a global effort to map all the genes in the human body—Jay's dream was to build the Human Diagnosis Project, a global effort to map the ways doctors use medical information to make diagnoses and other medical decisions. Just as Wikipedia was built by experts around the world who freely authored and edited encyclopedia articles that anyone could access online, the Human Diagnosis Project would be built by doctors around the world sharing and solving clinical cases.

When I came to understand Jay's vision, I realized how it could help the Ms. Sarahs of the world. In the near term, as our first doctors uploaded clinical cases that they had already solved, it would allow other doctors to learn from cases like Ms. Sarah's so that when they encountered patients with similar symptoms, they would know what to do. Later, as our community got larger, doctors—like the first one who saw Ms. Sarah—could post clinical cases they couldn't diagnose and get free help from other physicians around the world. Long term, Ms. Sarah herself would be able to type in her medical information and get input from doctors globally—and eventually, instantly receive a list of possible diagnoses and next steps in her care.

Inspired by the mission and seeing an opportunity to systematically solve a problem that had been vexing me for years, I took the plunge and left a job at an established company to join the team. We built a mobile app that doctors could use to post clinical cases for doctors around the world to practice diagnosing. As physicians contributed, the system recorded all of their data in a way that a machine could understand. By using artificial intelligence to analyze the data, we hoped to learn from it.

The challenges were many. The first one we confronted was convincing busy doctors to contribute their medical expertise to our system—and do so for free. Yet two years later, we had a community of 10,000 physician-contributors from over 80 countries. As I traveled to different conferences and meetings presenting our work, the question I would get over and over from incredulous healthcare leaders was: "We can't even get our doctors to show up for meetings. How are you getting doctors to participate? What's their incentive?"

What we found was that our system harkened back to what it means to be a physician. If you ask doctors why they went into medicine and why they keep practicing, you typically get three answers:

1. They love helping patients.

2. The camaraderie that comes from being in a noble profession.

3. The satisfaction of getting better at their craft.

For many of our participants, medicine had gotten away from that. The Human Diagnosis Project filled the void. Every moment on our system was spent doing what mattered most to doctors—helping patients, being part of a community with a broader mission, and boosting their own clinical expertise. At one of these meetings, Maureen Bisognano, a senior fellow at the Institute for Healthcare Improvement and its former CEO, gave me a better explanation: "What you've tapped into is the intrinsic motivation of professionals in medicine. It's the 3Ms: meaning, membership, and mastery."

The next challenge was to show that our system worked. Would doctors collaborating on our software get to accurate— and ideally better—results? To answer this, we partnered with a group of researchers at Harvard Medical School who were grappling with a similar question. Ateev Mehrotra and his team had created a set of what's called "clinical vignettes"—hypothetical patient cases meant to test the ability of a doctor to diagnose and treat medical problems. They had seen tremendous increases in the use of online symptom checkers like WebMD and wanted to understand how accurate they were. They entered the clinical vignettes into 20 different symptom checkers and found that the average symptom checker got the clinical vignette correct 34 percent of the time. Two out of three times, it got the diagnosis of very simple cases wrong![4]

Now the Harvard team was interested in understanding just how bad that was. While 34 percent seemed low, they didn't have a reference point. How would doctors fare on these same cases?

Together we fed the clinical vignettes they developed into our system and asked the doctors in our community to guess the diagnosis, much as they would if they were taking a medical school exam. Our software scored their responses, and as an additional step, automatically combined the diagnoses of multiple doctors into what we called a "collective opinion" and scored that too.

Not surprisingly, when the Harvard team ran the numbers, the data showed that individual doctors outperformed the symptom checkers. Doctors got the cases correct 72 percent of the time, more than twice as often as the symptom checkers. At least for now the jobs of doctors are safe![5]

But when our team went a step further to test the accuracy of the collective opinion compared to individual doctors, the results shocked us. When we combined the inputs of five or more doctors into a single diagnosis—effectively creating a virtual collaboration—the accuracy shot up from 72 percent to 85 percent. The results, moreover, demonstrated what scientists called a "dose response." As we combined the inputs of more and more doctors, the accuracy kept increasing—from two doctors (78 percent), to three doctors (83 percent), to five doctors (85 percent), to 10 doctors (93 percent). In medicine, as it turned out, many heads are better than one.[6]

Once we had built a large and growing physician community and proved the accuracy of the system, the third challenge was to get doctors to use it.

We had just been honored by the MacArthur Foundation—the organization that awards "genius" grants—as one of eight semifinalists for a $100 million prize designed to identify bold solutions that could change the world. Buoyed by their support, we decided to think bigger. Doctors around the world were using our system but doing so outside of day-to-day clinical practice. What if we could modify our app so doctors could use it to answer clinical questions in routine practice?

In the fall of 2018, after over a year of planning, pitching, and building, we were ready to launch. We had secured funding for a pilot from the Commonwealth Fund, one of the most respected healthcare foundations in the country. We had signed partnerships with nine clinics—from Hawaii, to New Mexico, to my own clinic in Washington, DC. And the early data was exciting—in a single 60-minute training session at a clinic in Chicago, we successfully signed up 80 percent of the physicians and got them using the app.

But months after the launch, the real-time dashboard we built to track usage seemed empty. Where beautiful red, blue, and green lines should have been streaking up and to the right, signaling usage increasing week over week, we saw only blank space. Doctors weren't using our app.

We had done everything right. And yet it had gone terribly wrong. Why weren't doctors using our app to ask clinical questions? What were we missing? We spent the next several months trying to fix the problem. But despite some modest victories, the pilot was largely a failure.

In our post mortem, what we learned was that the culture and demands of medicine had gotten in the way. Doctors didn't ask for help with their patients because they were worried that doing so would reveal what they didn't know.

The app also didn't work within their clinical workflow. It was outside of the electronic health record, which meant doctors had to waste precious time pulling up a second screen, either on their phone or on their internet browser. The responses were also too slow. They needed cases to be answered in minutes, while the patient was in the room; otherwise, it created extra work for them later.

The clinics also lacked incentives to push adoption. The doctors themselves were highly motivated by the 3Ms, but the administrators were not. While the clinics we worked with cared deeply about their patients, they ultimately had businesses to run. In fee-for-service medicine, there is no business model for improving the decisions doctors make, so it was hard for clinics to justify expending the resources it would take to enable our app to launch from their electronic health record or to sufficiently train and support doctors to use it day-to-day.

While the Human Diagnosis Project has been a resounding success and continues to scale around the world, it will take more than cutting edge technology and the goodwill of doctors to transform the healthcare system.

REALIZING THE VISION

As the Human Diagnosis Project pilot example showed, realizing the vision of collaborative care will require fundamental changes in culture, payment models, and care delivery.

Embracing the Idea That Healthcare Takes a Village

The shift to collaborative care will require us to free ourselves from the notion that healthcare is what happens between a single doctor and a single patient. From the first days of medical school, the idea of the physician as an individual hero is deeply ingrained in the identities of physicians. We hail the doctor who gets the diagnosis right, the surgeon who makes the lifesaving cut, and the ideal of being somebody's doctor.

Breaking the mental stranglehold will not be easy. But it may also be less difficult than we think, as I learned at Accolade. When I joined the organization, our care model for over 10 years was to "surround" the doctor visit: our nurses called members before they saw the doctor to help them prepare for the visit and then called them immediately after the visit to help them with next steps. When I started, I had a radical idea: What if our nurses could actually be "in" the visit? By asking patients to call us during the visit and put us on speakerphone, our nurses could listen in on the visit and give patients and doctors extra support in real time. As we prepared to test this idea, a major question lingered: Would doctors actually agree to it? Our worry was that doctors may covet their one-on-one time with patients and may be uncomfortable with a nurse who they don't know joining the conversation. The answer, however, from a pilot we conducted was a resounding "yes." Later, during the pandemic, when my mom got kidney stones out of town and I couldn't travel to be with her, I used the same approach to be "in" her visits. Time and again, I was pleasantly surprised when busy doctors, from ER physicians to urology specialists, agreed to dial me in so I could ask questions over the phone.

Part of the reason, I suspect, is that collaborative care has benefits for doctors, too. It's hard to talk about innovation and change in medicine today without acknowledging the problem of doctor burnout. The causes are multifactorial, but what I've seen firsthand is that collaboration has a role in restoring joy to clinical practice. Doctors who work in multidisciplinary clinics often say they'll never go back to solo practice. Attending doctors in academic medical centers look forward to case conferences and rounds. And I know firsthand from my clinic that patient care is more rewarding when family members and loved ones are involved.

Paying for the Right Care, Not for Visits

Medicine today largely pays for individual visits between a single patient and a single doctor. If two doctors see the same patient in the same visit, only one can bill for it. In fact, in some instances, two healthcare providers can't bill for two separate visits for the same patient on the same day. For example, many insurance companies won't reimburse clinics for providing medical services and mental health services on the same day. Integrating mental health seamlessly into primary care—which is exactly what we want to happen—is not allowed.

But the issue goes beyond payment for visits. Doctors can't bill for case conferences or tumor boards even though they have a significant impact on patient care. They also can't bill for informal consultations—what doctors often refer to as "curbside consults"—like when I worked in the hospital and used to call infectious disease experts to quickly verify the dose of an antibiotic I was prescribing. We insist on paying doctors for each time they help a patient, but then don't reimburse them for a significant proportion of that effort. The shift to bundled payments (in which health systems are paid a fixed amount of money for all the services they provide for a single condition) and the shift to capitated payments (in which health systems are given a fixed amount of money to provide all the care a patient needs) are a start.

Changes to payment are also needed to enable patients to get care wherever it makes the most sense for them—like Ms. Sarah was able to do. Ideally, doctors would be reimbursed both for in-person consultations like Ms. Sarah had and virtual consultations like the one in the hypothetical vision for her care. Employers and insurers should be able to contract for services anywhere in the country or enable patients to get fairly reimbursed for services from providers of their choice.

This goes against the current trend of insurance companies and employers creating narrower and narrower networks of doctors that patients can see without incurring a large co-pay. The concept of narrow networks makes sense in theory because they limit the network to doctors who are high quality and affordable. However, in reality, they don't work effectively because they measure quality by physician reputation (not condition-specific outcomes) and measure the price of discrete services (not total costs of care).

To get around this, some insurers and employers are purchasing second-opinion services that contract with high-quality specialists around the country. They then make it easy for their members to get a second opinion when they have a complex medical need or before undergoing an invasive and potentially avoidable procedure. We need more solutions like this.

Reorganizing Care Around Patients, Not Doctors

As I learned with the Human Diagnosis Project, existing clinical workflows present an enormous barrier to collaborative care. Changing them requires significant upfront investment, management, and training, as we've seen from examples where collaborative care has been effectively implemented. When NYC Health + Hospitals, the largest public health system in the United States, rolled out eConsults to expand access to specialty care for their uninsured and underinsured patients, they did a lot of groundwork first. They invested in expanding routine data collection to track and report progress, enhanced their electronic health record to support new clinical workflows, and cultivated clinical and administrative champions. In the process, they learned that consistent communication is essential so that primary care doctors, specialists, and patients understand the shift in expectations. They also realized that providers need to prepare to manage the short-term increase in workload that comes with transitioning from one care model to another.

The results were worth it. They found that 30 percent of specialist referrals could be handled by eConsult alone. This saved many patients the time and expense of a second doctor visit and cut down wait times for specialist input from several weeks or months to an average of just one week.[7]

STRATEGIC ACTIONS

The shift to collaborative care will break down the artificial silos in healthcare, enabling patients to benefit from greater expertise, better decision-making, and more informal and formal support. To unlock this potential, we need to move away from the one-to-one model of care between an individual doctor and an individual patient that has persisted in healthcare for so long. Doing so will require new payment models, delivery models, and tools that support collaboration in a way that creates value for each individual involved in the care process.

Here are some steps that each of us can take to accelerate our path to collaborative care and position ourselves and our organizations to succeed.

Patients, Caregivers, and Consumers of Care

- Have someone go with you to the doctor's office, even by phone. It can be as simple as calling a friend or family member and putting them on speakerphone during your visit.

- Find out if your employer or health insurance company offers a second opinion or centers of excellence program, so you know who to call if you ever have a serious diagnosis or medical issue.

- If you have a chronic condition, seek out peer support programs so you can get to know other patients like you and learn from their lived experience.

Physicians and Healthcare Professionals

- Seek out opportunities to get input on your tough cases from your peers. You'll learn a ton, connect more with your colleagues, and deliver better care in the process.

- Prompt your patients to bring their family members and friends to their visits, including by phone.

Healthcare Delivery Systems, Including Traditional and Technology Enabled

- Seek out new payment models that enable you to accelerate the transformation to collaborative care, such as electronic consults (e-consults) and risk-based payment.

- Invest in multidisciplinary clinics that simplify the patient experience, improve decision-making, and reduce physician burnout.

- Bring back case rounds, care conferences, and morbidity and mortality meetings (M&Ms) to foster a culture of collaboration.

- Track collaborations, such as curbside consults and participation in care conferences, in your physician productivity measures.

- Invest in messaging and communication platforms to make it simple and fast for your doctors and care teams to collaborate with one another.

Payers, Including Employers, Government Entities, and Health Plans

- Pay for e-consults, second-opinion services, and centers of excellence programs that improve patients' access to medical expertise.

- Use data on quality and outcomes to help match patients to the best doctors for their condition.

Policymakers

- Implement payment parity for virtual specialty care.

- Remove obstacles to patients receiving care from any doctor or healthcare delivery system in the country, particularly if those providers have demonstrated better outcomes and lower total costs of care.

- Invest in collaborative care models that integrate mental health in primary care settings, particularly in underserved communities.

Healthcare Investors and Entrepreneurs

Invest in and build companies that:

- Provide expert second opinions.

- Deliver e-consults and virtual specialty care.

- Provide tools for doctor-to-doctor, patient-to-caregiver, and patient-to-patient collaboration.

- Improve transparency on provider quality and expertise.

- Match patients to physicians based on their expertise and preferences.

CHAPTER 7

PERSONALIZED

ADDRESSING PATIENTS'
UNIQUE NEEDS AND
SOCIAL CONTEXTS

Three months into the pandemic, I saw a patient who brought me to tears.

It was in late April 2020, during the peak of the first wave of Covid-19. People were scared. The streets were empty, save for people getting essential goods. And those fortunate enough to do so were spending nearly all of their time holed up in their homes.

On my clinic schedule that day was a visit for diabetes follow-up. After weeks of seeing 20 to 30 patients a day with Covid-19, I was relieved to finally see a patient for something else.

From her record, I learned that Ms. Smith, as I'll call her, was a 62-year-old woman with a long-standing history of type 2 diabetes and peripheral nerve disease. Scanning her blood work over the past two years, I noted that her blood sugars had been controlled at certain times, but wildly elevated at others.

Multiple notes referred to her missing appointments, but they didn't say why.

As soon as I got her on the phone and introduced myself, she said: "Doctor, I really need your help with something." She explained that she was homeless. It had been almost a year since she had steady housing, and she was living in a shelter, which was overcrowded. She was certain that it was just a matter of time before she got Covid-19 and got it bad.

She had just learned about a program from the county, in which individuals at higher risk of Covid-19 could qualify to be moved to a hotel where they'd be able to socially distance more effectively. All they needed was a doctor's letter. She asked if I'd be willing to write one.

As she spoke, my heart sank. The very idea that someone in the wealthiest country on earth would be homeless and need a signature from me to get a safe and dignified place to stay was gut-wrenching. As soon as we hung up, I typed up and printed a letter detailing her medical history. My hands were shaking so hard that I could barely sign my name. It wasn't lost on me in the moment that this letter might be the most impactful prescription I would ever write.

On the drive home later that day, I couldn't stop thinking about Ms. Smith. I hadn't known she was homeless. It's only because she divulged that information to me that I was even aware of her precarious situation. Although I had heard of such hotel programs around the country, I wasn't aware that one was available in my own community.

How many more of my patients were homeless? How many more could I safely get to a hotel? How many more had needs that I could help address but wasn't? It was too much to bear. I pulled over and started crying.

After I composed myself, I began imagining how care should work for Ms. Smith and every patient who faced barriers to good health—what are called contextual barriers—like housing instability, food insecurity, joblessness, transportation issues, and domestic violence.

Here's what I envisioned: As soon as I pull up a patient's electronic health record, I see a list of contextual barriers prominently displayed next to their medical history, medication list, and vital signs. The list of barriers comes from multiple sources of information, including their address, demographic, and family information; routine surveys that ask them about their housing, financial, and social situations; and barriers identified in prior visits. The data is shown in a way that gives me insight into my patients' health. For example, rather than simply showing me someone's home address, the system links to publicly available data, such as census data to show me the financial health of the neighborhood they live in. Moreover, the insights are contextualized to the patient's health concerns. Pollen counts and air pollution levels are shown when I'm seeing a patient for asthma, but not when I'm treating a patient for back pain. In Ms. Smith's case, the home address she provided to our front desk staff is linked to a database of local homeless shelters, which generates a flag in her record indicating that she may be homeless.

Knowing the barriers a patient faces changes the care I provide. If I know a patient is between jobs, I'm sure to ask whether the medications I've prescribed fit within their budget. If I'm aware that a patient lives in an area with limited sidewalks, I counsel them on parks and shopping malls as safe places to exercise. When I ask Ms. Smith about her housing situation, she confirms that she is homeless and shares her worry about getting Covid-19.

The electronic health record puts a broad array of tools to address my patients' nonmedical needs at my fingertips. These extend beyond what's available within the healthcare system—to resources offered by the patient's employer, the government, and nonprofit and charitable organizations. With a click of a button,

I can then "prescribe" services like discount coupons for medications or transportation vouchers. In Ms. Smith's case, I ask whether she's willing to meet with a social worker and she agrees. The system dials a social worker into the visit. (No more having to remember dozens of different phone numbers!) After I explain the situation, she tells us about the hotel program and confirms Ms. Smith's eligibility. All I have to do is email her a letter and she'll take care of the rest.

Two days later her paperwork is accepted, and Ms. Smith has the most peaceful sleep she has had in months.

VISION OF PERSONALIZED CARE

This chapter is about the shift to *personalized care*, which we define as care that meets patients' individual needs and preferences. Just as personalized medicine tailors treatments to individuals' unique genetic profiles, personalized care tailors clinical guidance to individuals' unique contexts.

This vision of healthcare is one that recognizes that a person's social context is as important to their health as their biomedical context. In Ms. Smith's case, that context was homelessness. But every patient has a story and that story impacts their health. The story could be that they recently lost their job and can't afford their medications, that they have a chronically ill child at home and lack the time to care for themselves, or that they don't have stable transportation and often miss appointments.

Personalized care not only acknowledges social context, but also is systematically tailored to that context. The result is that patients receive care that fits into their lives rather than having to fit their lives into their care. No more scheduling appointments they can't make, prescribing medications they can't afford, and giving advice they can't follow. Patients will instead be provided with options that can help them balance their health needs with their financial, emotional, and family needs.

Personalized care is also more holistic. Doctors—myself included—tend to overmedicalize health. When patients have headaches, we prescribe pills rather than relaxation techniques; when they have chest pain, we order extensive cardiac workups instead of asking about stress. As a result, patients often miss out on a wide range of nonmedical approaches that could help address the root causes of their conditions.

This vision is rooted in the pioneering work of a compassionate physician and brilliant researcher named Saul Weiner. In a series of experiments, Saul and his colleagues revealed just how powerful context can be and how often it is missed in everyday clinical practice.

In one experiment, Saul's research team hired actors to portray patients with specific conditions and sent them to clinics all around Chicago. The doctors knew that some of the patients that they would see on a given day would be actors posing as patients, but they didn't know which ones.

One of the actors played the patient Aaron James, a 43-year-old man with asthma, who complains of worsening symptoms and mentions a list of medications he's taking, including a brand-name inhaler. "Aaron" made visits to 50 doctors in the Chicago area with the same story. What he didn't automatically reveal was his fictitious backstory: he wasn't actually taking his asthma medication as prescribed. He had recently lost his job and could no longer afford to use the expensive inhaler every day. However, at every visit, he would drop a hint: "Boy, it's been tough since I lost my job."

The study was designed to determine how often the doctor would pick up on the hint—what Dr. Weiner calls a contextual red flag. To measure that, the patient-actor secretly audiorecorded the visit. Then researchers listened to the recordings and assessed whether the doctor's ultimate plan for the patient reflected his real problem—that he couldn't afford his asthma medication.

The results were fascinating. Dr. Weiner and his team found that doctors failed to provide appropriate "contextualized" care 78 percent of the time. In one audiorecording, the doctor's response to "Boy, it's been tough since I lost my job" was "I'm sorry to hear that. It's been a rough economy lately. Do you have allergies?" The result was that Aaron left the doctor's office with a prescription for a higher dosage of the unaffordable medication and a referral for an expensive lung-function test that he didn't need.

The 22 percent of doctors who provided appropriate care simply asked the patient how the job loss was affecting his care—what Dr. Weiner calls a contextual probe—and incorporated what they had learned into the care plan. As an example, in another audiorecording, the doctor's reply was "I'm sorry to hear that. How has it been tough? Is it affecting your healthcare?" It turned out just that was enough. Aaron left the doctor's office with a prescription for a much less costly generic inhaler—one he could afford.[1]

When I heard about Saul's research, my first thought was that I could have easily been the first doctor (and not just because I used to practice in Chicago). How often have I seen a patient and in the rush of the visit completely missed a contextual red flag?

What's remarkable about Saul's experiments is that nearly all the patients got biomedically appropriate care. Clinical guidelines for asthma state that for someone like Aaron James with uncontrolled symptoms, doctors should increase the dose of their medication or add another medication to their regimen. And that's exactly what many of the doctors did. And yet, that's not at all what the patient needed.

These outcomes weren't just bad for the patient; they also were bad for the system. In a follow-up study, Dr. Weiner and his team found that contextual errors resulted in unnecessary tests and treatments that cost the healthcare system an average of over $231 per visit.[2] But those were just the direct costs of the visit itself. The indirect costs were likely much higher. It's not hard to imagine Aaron James winding up in the emergency room for uncontrolled asthma and racking up an expensive ER bill.

REALIZING THE VISION

Personalized care has a number of major implications for care delivery.

Integrating Data on Social Needs

When it comes to social and behavioral factors that influence health, most doctors ask patients about smoking and alcohol use, but that's about it. To realize the vision of personalized care, we need to go beyond this. Part of the solution is making better use of the data we already have. I have a home address for every patient I see, but my electronic health record doesn't automatically translate their address into something that helps me understand my patients better. Does the patient live in a neighborhood with high rates of asthma? Is theirs a zip code with a lower life expectancy?

We will also need to collect more data on social needs from patients themselves. One such tool is a brief, standardized screening instrument developed by the Institute of Medicine, which poses 12 questions about race and ethnicity, gender, education, stress, physical activity, social connection, and partner violence.[3]

Once we have the data, how can we use it to improve care? Dr. Weiner's research may soon have the answer. Saul is currently leading a research study to determine how contextual data can be incorporated in the electronic health record to improve clinical decision-making. His intervention has three parts:

1. Patients are asked about social needs, and any positive findings are displayed in the electronic health record in a "contextual care box" next to the patients' vital signs and medications.

2. The electronic health record mines its own data to automatically identify contextual red flags to add to the box—for example, that a patient has been in the ER multiples times, is not refilling their medications, or has missed appointments.

3. The electronic health record provides doctors guidance on how to address these barriers—for example, by prescribing a pill box to organize their medications or referring them to a social worker—and automatically documents it in the patient's record.[4]

"What we're trying to do is automate and simplify so that physicians get contextual information—both from the patient and the medical record—at the point of care," he explained.

Training the Workforce

Decision support won't be enough. We need doctors and care teams who know how to practice personalized care. We need a healthcare workforce that listens for contextual red flags and then asks the next question to understand how those factors are impacting the patient's health.

Here again Saul's research provides valuable insights. In another study, he worked with six clinics in the Veterans Administration to audiorecord over 4,000 real-life patient visits and then used the data to give doctors regular feedback and coaching on how well they contextualized care. Over a two-year period, the rate of doctors contextualizing care increased from 67 to 72 percent, resulting in an estimated savings of $25 million compared to the program cost of $337,000.[5]

Saul believes that recording patient visits should be mandated: "It's crazy that our healthcare system has been studying and measuring quality of care for decades with absolutely no data from the actual delivery of care."

Expanding the Care Team and Services Available

Training may not always be enough. In a busy clinical practice, doctors may need new types of health professionals who have more time to understand patients' contextual barriers and have specialized skills and training to help address them.

For example, Health Leads is a nonprofit organization that places undergraduate students in the waiting rooms of hospitals and health centers to assess food, housing, and other social needs and connect patients to local resources.[6] Other examples include the use of community health workers in neighborhoods and churches, in-house attorneys to address housing and legal issues, and even interprofessional teams of nurses, occupational therapists, and handymen to help older adults achieve independence.[7]

Personalized care may also require new types of interventions and services to offer patients. The United Kingdom has pioneered a model called "social prescribing" that enables doctors to prescribe not only medical tests and treatments but also social activities. In their model, a primary care doctor refers patients to a link worker, who then partners with the patient to identify nonmedical services they would benefit from—ranging from coffee chats to singing groups to meditation. One of their case studies is of a woman whose depression left her bedbound. After being prescribed art therapy, she recovered and now works for the national health service promoting mental health services to others. In her own words: "I still have the mental illness, but I manage it rather than it managing me. . . . To say art saved my life is not a phrase I use lightly, it saved it yes, but it transformed it beyond any recognition to anything I have ever had before."[8]

Connecting the Social Services Ecosystem

In addition to expanding the resources available to frontline care teams, we need to also integrate the tools and services we have into our clinical workflows. In my clinic, many of those resources are scribbled on sticky notes and stuck on our walls, or are in the minds of individual social workers and practitioners. This means that when the information is needed, it's often hard to find, and if you're lucky enough to locate it, it's usually outdated.

I talked to Marc Rabner, a pediatrician and expert in public health at CRISP—the health information exchange I mentioned in Chapter 4—shortly after my phone call with Ms. Smith, my patient living in a homeless shelter. Marc had a number of ideas for how we can better serve patients like her in the future. To begin, we can compile digital resource directories where doctors and care teams can quickly look up what resources are available to patients, what services they provide, what their hours of operation are, what languages they speak, and what their eligibility requirements are—and have all of that information in one place. Then we need to use the directories to make closed-loop referrals, meaning when we refer patients to those resources, we get data back on whether the patient actually received the service and ideally whether and how they benefited from it.

With that kind of system, I could have easily found the hotel housing program for Ms. Smith, even if she or I weren't aware of it, and then automatically referred her through my electronic health record. The system would then help me track her progress from receipt of my referral (I never quite know if my faxes get through!) to acceptance into the program to the first day she checked in. The system would also alert me when her program status needed to be renewed, so I could write another medical letter to keep her safe and sound.

There is still a major hurdle to achieving the kind of system Marc and I envisioned—government regulations like HIPPA and FERPA (Family Educational Rights and Privacy Act), which prevent sharing information without the explicit consent of patients or parents.

"We have to have a more accessible way of patients consenting to their data sharing—while also providing the right context and having them understand why it's important for them to share that information—so that they can be in charge of their data. That means finding that right balance between patient privacy and public health/clinical care," Marc says.

Putting It All Together

Effectively realizing the vision of personalized care will require implementing more than one of the recommendations I presented earlier. Simply collecting data about patients' social needs without giving doctors more resources to address them is unlikely to have an impact. But that doesn't mean that the implementation needs to be perfect.

At Accolade, all of our frontline care teams undergo training on personalized care. Dr. Weiner's research is ingrained in a model we call LEARN2:

Listen with empathy.

Engage with reflection, validation, and support.

Assess the needs of others and how we can help.

Resolve issues by following through and meeting commitments.

INfluence others by providing options and allowing for choice.

ENhance by sharing your experience and expertise.

But training is just the starting point. LEARN2 is also part of our culture. We start all of our company-wide town halls and monthly management meetings with a member story that highlights a recent success case. The "John" story of attempted suicide in Chapter 4 is an example. In addition, we record our calls and periodically review them with our frontline care teams to provide feedback on how well they are implementing LEARN2.

A study done by Saul Weiner and his team found that our teams are good at this. In fact, it showed that our teams are more likely than doctors to act on contextual barriers. When Saul's team compared recordings from three sources—two groups of physician/patient visits and one group of phone calls with Accolade health assistants—they found that Accolade's frontline care teams considered contextual factors in 82 percent of patients' treatment plans, compared to 59 percent for one group of physicians and 63 percent for the other.[9]

Our homegrown technology platform also supports the model. Every patient record has a section for barriers of care prominently displayed next to the patient's list of conditions and medications. It also prompts our frontline care teams to ask about barriers, such as screening for depression.

Our system is a work in progress. Many of the tools we use to address contextual barriers, such as prescription discount or food assistance programs, live on separate websites. The resources are curated and updated regularly, but they'd likely be used more often if we integrated them into specific care pathways on our platform. We also don't consistently collect race and ethnicity data from our customers, or survey the whole population on social needs, which would yield additional contextual red flags for our frontline care teams to act on.

STRATEGIC ACTIONS

The shift to personalized care will help address many of the root causes of poor health by contextualizing care to individuals' social needs. Personalized care also offers a pragmatic approach for improving health equity within the context of individual patient care. To unlock this potential, we need to move beyond the biomedical model of medicine and integrate new kinds of data, resources, and professionals into clinical care.

Here are some steps that all of us can take to accelerate our path to personalized care and position ourselves and our organizations to succeed.

Patients, Caregivers, and Consumers of Care

* Expect more from your doctor and your healthcare provider. Ask them how they link patients to nonmedical services like financial assistance, social support, and community organizations. If they look at you blankly, that's a bad sign.

* If you are having trouble paying for your medical care or getting to your appointments—or having issues at work or at home—tell your doctor. Our health is closely tied to our overall well-being, and often doctors have access to resources that can help you.

Physicians and Healthcare Professionals

* Audiorecord at least one patient visit a week (with permission from your patient) and listen to it. How long before you interrupted the patient? Did you miss any contextual red flags? Were your recommendations personalized to their individual situation?

Healthcare Delivery Systems, Including Traditional and Technology Enabled

* Review your quality and outcome data by race, ethnicity, and economic status to understand health disparities within your patient population.

* Integrate social determinants of health data into your electronic health record and implement processes to ask patients about their social needs at least once per year. A

great place to start is the Institute of Medicine instrument referenced earlier.

- Invest in care teams and tools that make it simple and quick for clinicians to act on contextual barriers they identify within a busy visit or hospital shift.

- Partner in new ways with community-based organizations that make it easy to refer patients to them—ideally within the electronic health record—and get data back on whether the referral happened and what outcomes were achieved.

- Implement a system to record patient visits and measure whether your providers pick up on contextual red flags and give them feedback on it.

Payers, Including Employers, Government Entities, and Health Plans

- When a healthcare delivery organization, vendor, or potential partner shares data with you, ask, "Can you send me this data by race, ethnicity, and household income?" In return, share the data you have on your members' social context so they can provide these analyses.

- Invest in partners, resources, and tools that address the social determinants of health.

- Expand risk adjustment methods so that providers receive higher payments for patients with greater social needs.

Policymakers

- Promote workforce development for community health workers, peer counselors, and nontraditional healthcare professionals who can help patients with health-related social needs. For example, establish accreditation models for these professionals and integrate them into new payment models.

- Develop standards for social determinants of health data, including screening, diagnosis, planning, and interventions to enable interoperability and closed loop referrals between healthcare providers and community organizations.

- Invest in social services like job assistance, food pantries, housing, transportation, education, and legal aid. Then, critically, invest in making data about such services up to date and widely available to healthcare providers.

- Expand medical home and accountable care organization definitions to include community organizations and nonmedical social service partners to create a holistic "neighborhood" of accountable entities.

Healthcare Investors and Entrepreneurs

Invest in and build companies that make it easier for doctors, care teams, and caregivers to personalize care by:

- Streamlining the collection of data on social determinants of health.

- Integrating social determinants of health data into electronic health records.

- Developing actionable insights from social determinants of health data.

- Facilitating closed-loop referrals with community organizations and social service providers.

- Connecting the ecosystem of medical and social service providers.

CHAPTER 8

RESPONSIVE

USING DATA AND EVIDENCE
TO GUIDE DECISION-MAKING

A few years ago, I took care of a 62-year-old woman, an immigrant from Somalia whom I'll call Mrs. Ibrahim. On her long list of medical conditions was hepatitis C, a chronic infectious disease caused by a virus that affects the liver. She was diagnosed years earlier in her home country and had never received treatment.

When I noted it during her first visit, I fell back to my old habits from residency. Hepatitis C wasn't a condition that could be treated very effectively then. The available medications were often too expensive for patients or not indicated for their stage of the disease. So I set her hepatitis C aside, focusing instead on addressing her health concerns, which were unrelated to hepatitis C, and building a relationship with her and her family, who were new to America and were generally mistrustful of the US health-care system.

It wasn't until eight months later, when I stumbled across a news article about the costs of the newer hepatitis C drugs, that I suddenly remembered that I had a patient who might be a candidate for treatment. (I seldom encountered patients with hepatitis C in my clinic.)

I spent the next two hours devouring the latest journal articles and clinical guidelines on hepatitis C. The more I read, the more evident it became that Mrs. Ibrahim was a candidate for treatment and that with treatment, she had a high chance of cure.

To confirm my thinking, I called a colleague, an infectious disease doctor who specializes in the treatment of HIV/AIDS, hepatitis C, and other chronic infections. When I explained Mrs. Ibrahim's situation, she immediately said, "Oh, of course, this patient should have been treated months ago." I felt sick to my stomach. I had let my patient down. I had let her family down. If she had a better doctor, her hepatitis C would have been gone by now.

I scheduled Mrs. Ibrahim for an appointment and asked her daughter to join us. I explained to them that since she had been diagnosed with hepatitis C a decade ago, a new treatment had become available. She hadn't yet developed any liver complications from her infection, but she might in the future. Treatment was recommended and may in fact cure her condition. They were thrilled at the news—especially Mrs. Ibrahim's daughter who admitted she had been worried about her mom's infection for some time.

But I wasn't finished yet. With a lump forming in my throat, I told them that I had also made a huge mistake. I should have brought this to their attention months ago, and if I had, she might have gotten rid of her infection already.

They refused to accept my apology. Seeing tears well up in my eyes, Mrs. Ibrahim, who often reminded me of my own grandmother, said: "You are my doctor. Before, you were not. We take this journey together."

○—○—○

I have reflected on Mrs. Ibrahim many times in the years since. I usually beat myself up over it. I failed my patient. I should have kept up on hepatitis C better and treated her sooner.

But on my better days, I see it more as a systems problem. It shouldn't be on doctors alone to ensure that care is evidence-based and up to date. My electronic health record shouldn't just be documenting my decisions after the fact; it should be actively helping me make the right decisions. My clinic provides me with ongoing training, but often not on topics most relevant to my learning needs. Insurance companies are quick to send me a letter when I order a treatment that they think a patient doesn't need (they are usually wrong), but they seldom reach out when a patient isn't on a treatment that they do need. We need a better system of care—one that ensures that patients receive the best of what medicine has to offer each and every time.

This chapter is about the shift to *responsive care*, which I define as care that is evidence-based and up to date with the latest clinical guidelines and scientific research. Each year about three million scientific articles are published.[1] Every couple of years new clinical practice guidelines are released that instruct doctors on how to diagnose and treat nearly every major disease. Doctors also have to keep up with FDA advisories and warnings. A couple of years ago, a very common medication for high blood pressure produced by a single drug company, Teva Pharmaceuticals, was found to have a harmful contaminant, prompting the FDA to issue a recall.[2] And yet months later, I still saw new patients who were taking the medication.

A well-cited statistic in medicine is that, on average, it takes 17 years for a new evidence-based treatment to reach mainstream clinical practice.[3] It's worth pausing on that. That means that when you see a doctor in 2020, you are getting care from 2003. To put that in perspective, in 2003 the iPhone hadn't yet come out and Blockbuster was where we went to rent movies!

VISION FOR RESPONSIVE CARE

What if healthcare worked like this: You've come to see your doctor about a flare-up of rheumatoid arthritis (RA). As your doctor is asking you how you're doing, a message pops up on his screen. Based on your age, medical history, and recent lab results, there's a new treatment for RA that, according to a recent paper in *The New England Journal of Medicine,* may significantly improve your health.

Your doctor has never prescribed the treatment before, as it was just recently approved by the FDA. However, just a few weeks earlier, he participated in a weekly clinical conference in which his colleagues weighed the pros and cons of starting the treatment in three of their patients with a regional expert in rheumatoid arthritis.

Before he prescribes it, you and your doctor talk about whether this treatment makes sense for you. He then sends you home with reading materials and a video made by a national patient advocacy organization to help you understand the medication. Since this is a new medication, he is unsure of some of the practical considerations of starting it. The side effects, which are rare, range from infections to blood clots. Which side effects should he warn you about? If you start to have one, will it go away on its own or should he stop the treatment? After discussing your case at the next clinical conference, he feels much more comfortable proceeding. A couple of days later, you both agree to start the medication.

As soon as your doctor orders the treatment in his electronic health record, your medical information is securely and anonymously shared, with your permission, with a national patient registry. Your information complements data from clinical trials and helps doctors and patients understand the benefits of the treatment in the real-world and study rare side effects that may have gone undetected in a clinical trial.

As evidence of the effectiveness and safety of the treatment in patients like you accumulates, the American College of

Rheumatology (ACR) updates its clinical guidelines: they now recommend that most patients with your condition receive this treatment.

Soon your doctor receives a report from the ACR that shows the percentage of his patients with RA on this treatment compared to his peers. The report suggests he is behind the curve.

Within a couple minutes, using his electronic health record, your doctor generates a list of patients with RA who aren't on the treatment and sends a task to his front desk staff to schedule them for follow-up appointments.

Within weeks, many more of your doctor's patients—and patients around the country—are benefitting from the treatment, improving outcomes for thousands of patients like you.

o—o—o

Compare the preceding vision to the way medicine actually works today.

My super-expensive electronic health record is little more than a glorified electronic notepad. I don't get helpful alerts about recent clinical breakthroughs. When I type a symptom or a disease, nothing pops up. No guidance on what questions to ask, what tests to consider, or what treatments to prescribe. It's like typing into a word processor. The few exceptions to this are actually more annoying than they are helpful—for example, the alerts that needlessly warn me about medication interactions. The electronic health record is the embodiment of Aesop's boy who cried wolf—its warnings come so frequently and unnecessarily that we routinely disregard them even when they may be alerting us to true potential dangers.

Clinics like mine lack a systematic approach to training. They typically host educational sessions once a month. The clinic closes for half a day, and over stale bagels and weak coffee, doctors cover one or two educational topics. Often, these sessions are not relevant to my practice. Topics are chosen haphazardly, based more on the interests of my peers than on our patients' needs or on objective data showing where we need to improve. Moreover, the teaching methods are antiquated. We turn off the lights, stare at a PowerPoint deck, and passively listen to a medical-school-style lecture. At the end of the presentation, we may walk through two or three patient cases. This is often the most engaging part, but the cases are usually hypothetical, not based on actual patients we've encountered in our clinic. There is little opportunity for discussion or reflection on how to apply what we learned into practice.

The feedback I receive in clinic is narrow. Often, it is based on a review of a handful of my patients—and even then, it relies on what I wrote in the chart, which may or may not reflect what actually happened. Missing is objective data on my overall practice patterns.

Every week I get *JAMA* and *The New England Journal of Medicine* mailed to my home. Sometimes I read these medical journals, but often I don't. Even when I learn about a condition that is directly applicable to my practice, I rely on memory to guide me the next time I see a patient with it, which may be months away.

Every year I am required to complete a certain number of hours of continuing medical education (CME), which involves sitting through lectures or watching modules online and then answering multiple-choice questions to test my knowledge. Like my clinic educational sessions, CME usually isn't based on actual cases or directly applicable to my practice.

Every 10 years I have to sit for a recertification exam in my specialty. A decade is a wide gap, considering the pace of change in medicine. Although some medical boards, including my own, are beginning to experiment with more frequent exams, the test is largely of my memory rather than my actual practice. I can get every question right but not actually do those things in clinical practice. At the end of the test, all I see is "pass" or "fail." I don't get any actionable feedback like "You prescribed a 10-year-old medication for hepatitis C when a newer, more effective medication is now available."

Our system for ensuring that medical care is up to date and evidence-based can be largely summed up this way: it relies on memory and goodwill—the memory to recall what I learn as medicine changes and the goodwill to apply it to the care of each and every patient. It's no surprise then that it takes 17 years to update clinical practice.

REALIZING THE VISION

The vision I laid out exists in various forms in medicine today. While I don't know of a single health system that has all of the elements I described, each of the four elements exists to a degree in different health systems. Here are some examples and insights from those experiences.

Clinical Decision Support

As I'm typing a patient's condition or prescribing a medication, the electronic health record should inform me of the latest science and evidence-based guidelines. At Accolade, the software system used by our nurses contains over 500 different evidence-based assessments. If a patient is calling about a cough, the nurse pulls up an assessment in which the first question asks if the patient has difficulty breathing. If the patient calls about back pain, it asks if the patient had a recent fall or accident. These assessments are updated periodically as guidelines change. In addition, we can manually update the assessments whenever a more urgent change is required, something we needed to do during the pandemic.

As we started triaging the first cases of Covid-19, my team noticed a major problem. If a patient called in for Covid-19, our nurses would pull up a Covid-19 assessment that included evidence-based questions about the virus. But if a patient called in for cough or fever and didn't mention Covid-19, the assessment didn't prompt our nurses to ask about Covid-19 and possible exposures. So we manually modified our assessments, adding questions from the CDC. Within minutes of hitting "save," the assessments went live across our software system, better equipping hundreds of nurses to provide evidence-based guidance for over a million people.

Critically, as we implement clinical decision support, we need to ensure that we are not only responsive to the latest evidence-based guidelines but also responsive to the needs of patients. There is a danger that as we standardize care, the practice of medicine will be reduced to a series of check boxes. It will nearly always be important for these care pathways to be considered suggestions, not mandates, and to allow for clinical judgment and tailoring to individual patient circumstances.

Patient Registries

Although health systems have invested hundreds of millions of dollars in electronic health records, they are notoriously difficult to extract data from. During the pandemic, public health officials couldn't get access to the data they needed. How many patients were hospitalized with Covid-19? What percent of Covid-19 patients were African American or Latino? What treatments were associated with better outcomes? The irony was that nearly all of this data was available in an electronic format somewhere in the country. We just couldn't get to it.

Perhaps the best example of what is possible comes from a national patient registry of cystic fibrosis, an inherited disorder that causes severe damage to the lungs and other organs of the body starting in childhood. With support from the Cystic Fibrosis Foundation, over 130 accredited care centers for cystic fibrosis use a common system for storing and sharing data about their patients. The registry allows them not only to capture much more structured data on symptoms, treatments, and outcomes but also to share that data across centers. Researchers can then use the data to understand which treatments are working and which aren't and to hypothesize about new treatments and protocols that could be used in other cystic fibrosis patients. The capabilities of the system actually go beyond the vision I shared earlier. Not only does the system recommend patients for certain treatments, but it also notifies doctors and families about new clinical trials for which patients may be eligible.[4]

Partially as a result, patients with cystic fibrosis have seen a remarkable improvement in median life expectancy: from age 10 in the 1960s when the first registry was set up at Babies and Children's Hospital in Cleveland, to age 18 in the 1970s, to well over age 40 today.[5]

Imagine the impact such a system might have had on Covid-19! Had we had access to this kind of data, we may have discovered new treatments sooner and reduced the terrible morbidity and mortality from the pandemic.

Telementoring

Telementoring—specialists sharing their experience and expertise with generalists online—is the brainchild of Dr. Sanjeev Arora, a liver specialist at the University of New Mexico Health Sciences Center in Albuquerque. His model, called Project ECHO (Extension for Community Healthcare Outcomes), dates to 2003 when Sanjeev saw patient after patient come to the hospital with preventable complications from hepatitis C, the condition that affected Mrs. Ibrahim. Sanjeev was frustrated that he could serve only a fraction of the patients who needed his expertise. There were only so many hepatitis C specialists in the state. But he realized that these patients had primary care doctors who could provide this care, if only he could find a way to train them. Soon ECHO was born to do just that.

Today, there are hundreds of ECHO sites around the world where doctors and healthcare professionals learn how to manage a wide range of clinical conditions from hepatitis C and tuberculosis to diabetes and opiate use disorders. Doctors sign up for a clinical topic, which is facilitated by one or more experts.

Each week they participate in a video conference during which they present cases from their own practices, and experts provide guidance on how best to manage them. As a result, doctors are exposed to a far greater number of cases than they would otherwise be. The mentorship and support of expert clinicians drives their experiential learning and helps them gain confidence.

And ECHO works. In a paper published in *The New England Journal of Medicine*, Sanjeev and colleagues studied over 400 hepatitis C patients across New Mexico, comparing the outcomes of patients treated by specialists like himself to those of patients treated by generalists at an ECHO site. What they found was that sustained viral response—a near-term measure of successful treatment for hepatitis C—was achieved in 57.5 percent of patients treated by specialists compared to 58.2 percent of patients treated in the community with ECHO.[6]

A key insight from ECHO is that for responsive care to be effective, doctors need to change their behavior—and that behavior change seldom occurs from knowledge alone. For Mrs. Ibrahim, my hepatitis C patient, I knew what the right treatment was, but I didn't feel comfortable prescribing it until I had talked to another doctor. Although we claim to understand this, medical educators continue to give lectures to train doctors, hospitals send out emails with clinical updates to change practice, and insurance companies use "pay for performance" programs to improve quality. Instead, what we need is to use behavioral science—and where possible, real human connections—to help doctors improve.

As Sanjeev Arora shared with me when I asked him why ECHO works, "The secret to ECHO is building community, respectful interactions, and love."

Physician Scorecards

The idea of giving doctors feedback on their individual practice patterns has been tried by a number of organizations. Perhaps none have been as effective as a study done by a mentor of mine, Marty Makary, a surgeon and researcher at Johns Hopkins. Using a national data set of Medicare patients, Marty and his colleagues analyzed a very common surgical procedure used to treat skin cancer called Mohs microsurgery.

The ingenuity of Mohs surgery is that it allows the surgeon to check if the surgery is a success while the patient is still in the operating room. Rather than a single incision, which risks removing too much good skin and causing deformities or removing too little and not removing all of the cancer, Mohs enables surgeons to operate in stages and, at each stage, to check whether the tissue that was removed is cancer-free or not.[7]

There are guidelines to help Mohs surgeons decide whether or not another stage is necessary, but as always in medicine, individual judgment comes into play. It's up to the surgeon in the heat of an operation to decide what the right call is. There are also economic factors involved. Because more stages require more time, surgeons get paid more, the greater number of stages they perform.

What Marty and his team realized is that while judging individual cases is hard, you can assess a physician's overall practice pattern. If you look at 100 cases done by a Mohs surgeon and see that he has consistently billed for more stages than his peers, you might reasonably conclude the surgeon is practicing outside of the bounds of medicine.

So Marty and his team looked for statistical outliers in the data and then partnered with the American College of Mohs Surgery to send a letter to the outlier surgeons in their membership. The letter reiterated national guidelines about Mohs surgery and included a graph that plotted each outlier surgeon's practice patterns against those of their peers.

Marty and his team had no idea what would happen next. It was an experiment, after all. Would doctors actually open the letter? Would they read it? Would they do anything with the information?

The results startled them. What they found was that outlier surgeons reduced the number of stages by 83 percent. Through a simple letter in the mail, they were able to reduce inappropriate care, save Medicare $11 million—a sum that grew to $21 million in the follow-up analysis—and put more patients on the path toward getting the right care.[8]

One key to building a responsive system, Marty taught me, is to view inappropriate care as a systems issue. In his words, "When I see an outlier physician . . . I don't view them as a bad doctor, but as a doctor who needs help." That's the kind of system I would like to practice in and one that would have served my patient with hepatitis C much better.

More than anything, though, building a responsive system is about culture change. Marty reminded me that change begins with how we recruit people into medicine. In interviews he focuses on the demeanor of candidates to identify those who will become great doctors: How well do they listen? Do they ask questions? Are they interested in continual learning? "The greatest mark of a great doctor is their humility—the willingness to say, 'I don't know,'" he says.

STRATEGIC ACTIONS

The shift to responsive care can increase equitable access to high-quality care by reducing the time it takes for medical discoveries and evidence-based guidelines to be incorporated into clinical practice. But if not done well, it risks overburdening doctors or limiting their ability to adapt care to the needs of individual patients.

Here are some steps that all of us can take to accelerate our path to responsive care and position ourselves and our organizations to succeed.

Patients, Caregivers, and Consumers of Care

- Trust but verify. Ask your doctor, "Can you show me the clinical guidelines your recommendation is based on?"

- Seek out trusted sources of health information, such as the CDC, US Preventive Services Task Force, and physician societies to verify that the care you are receiving is evidence-based and up to date.

Physicians and Healthcare Professionals

- Sign up for an email or app-based service that regularly sends you the latest clinical guidelines with commentary from experts in your field. I use *Journal Watch* from *The New England Journal of Medicine*.

- Make evidence-based medicine a topic of conversation with your peers. Asking "Have you read any good papers lately?" is a good place to start. Better yet, start a journal club, care conference, or informal Friday case rounds over lunch or coffee, as an enjoyable way to spend time with your peers and keep learning.

Healthcare Delivery Systems, Including Traditional and Technology Enabled

- Measure variations in care across physicians, benchmarked where possible, and give physicians feedback on their individual performance.

- Implement clinical care pathways within your electronic health record with physician input at every step of the process.

- Invest in clinical decision support tools and track and optimize their use by physicians.

- Sign up for Project ECHO.[11] Pick a condition that your doctors are most excited to learn about and expand from there.

Payers, Including Employers, Government Entities, and Health Plans

- Demand that traditional and technology-enabled healthcare delivery organizations have processes in place to review, implement, and measure adherence to evidence-based protocols.

- Provide data to physicians to understand and improve their individual performance relative to their peers.

Policymakers

- Create incentives for health systems to invest in advanced patient queries, care pathways, and electronic disease registries.

- Provide grants and technical assistance to health systems to implement programs for retraining their health workforce like Project ECHO, particularly in low-income and rural communities where access to specialists is most limited.

- Invest in patient disease registries like the Cystic Fibrosis Foundation's through grants to healthcare delivery organizations that require the data to be standardized and open.

- Require digital health companies seeking FDA approval to demonstrate processes for ensuring use of up-to-date clinical guidelines.

- Convene physicians and medical stakeholders to design individual physician-level measures of evidence-based medicine and appropriateness of care for the purposes of feedback, not payment or punitive measures.

Healthcare Investors and Entrepreneurs

Invest in and build companies that:

- Reimagine the electronic health record and give doctors a more intuitive and customizable interface to their electronic health record.

- Digitize clinical guidelines and enable smarter clinical decision support.

- Measure adherence to evidence-based practice.

- Gamify medical education.

- Build communities of doctors to support case-based learning and spread evidence-based practice.

PART III

DECENTRALIZED

n the spring of 2019, during a brief stint at the World Bank, I traveled to Mozambique to review the country's community health worker program. The program trained laypeople, often with little more than an eighth-grade education, to go from household to household, registering pregnant women for prenatal care, advising on family-planning options, and diagnosing and treating malaria.

My role was to conduct an assessment of the program and inform the design of a formal World Bank evaluation that would start in a few months. The stakes were high: a favorable evaluation would unlock the equivalent of tens of millions of US dollars from the Mozambique government for the future scale-up of the program.

It was up to me to decide how to spend my two-day visit. Rather than stay in Maputo, the capital city, reviewing reports and sitting through PowerPoint presentations, I wanted to observe a community health worker on the job. If I could assess even one community health worker, perhaps I could get my head around how to assess the quality of an entire country of community health workers. Little did I realize then that the community health worker I was about to observe would actually teach me far more about delivering high-quality care than I could hope to teach her.

After a brief overnight stay in Maputo and a quick coffee at our World Bank offices to meet our staff on the ground, I rushed off to the airport to catch a flight to the region of Inhambane, an hour to the north. From the plane, the sprawling city of Maputo quickly gave way to fertile fields and then to flooded plains. Just weeks before my trip, two massive cyclones had hit the country, displacing over 160,000 people and killing hundreds.[1] I thought to myself, how can a community health worker even do her job in such conditions? I would soon find out.

The next morning, a small team of us traveled by car from the regional capital to the village where I would conduct my observation. City roads led to wide highways, which then led to town roads and then finally to a dirt road, on which our jeep traveled for nearly an hour, bumping this way and that as we wound ourselves into the heart of the Mozambiquan countryside. We finally arrived. Standing amid the tall grass, hours away by foot from the nearest hospital or town center, I immediately understood the need for community health workers to physically extend the reach of hospitals and clinics into the community.

We arrived outside a small batch of thatched dwellings. Standing in the shade of a tall tree in the 90-degree heat was our community health worker, formally known as an *agente polivalente elementar*, or APE (pronounced "a-pesh"). The young woman, whom I'll call Ashanti, was smartly dressed in a dark green vest and a backpack in which she carried her medical supplies and goods.

Ashanti was accompanied by an elderly gentleman, who was the village leader. The community had a voice in selecting who would be the first line of defense for their health and welfare, and he was proud to tell us he had served on the committee that elected Ashanti as their APE.

My first question to Ashanti was, "How do you know which patients to visit on a given day?" She answered in Portuguese, and as we waited for the translation, she picked up a stick from under the tree and began to sketch out in the dirt what appeared to be a map. Pointing at the map, she explained where her catchment area started and ended, how many households she was responsible for, and which parts were poorer and had more health issues.

Then still answering my first question, she reached into her pocket and retrieved a well-worn cell phone encased in a dusty plastic jacket. She opened up a software application and showed me her task list. The list helped her prioritize households based on the ages of the family members and their health issues. Households with young children and pregnant mothers were visited more often. Households with malaria required immediate follow-up.

I then asked, "How do you know what to do for a child with fever?" (Malaria is endemic in Mozambique and rates of death in children under age five are still far behind the goals set by the World Health Organization.)[2] Once again, she pulled out her phone, and with a couple of taps showed me a clinical workflow for fever. Each screen prompted her to ask a series of questions and record her observations, like the child's temperature or rate of breathing. To give me a full demonstration, my colleague from the World Bank pretended to be the sick child's caregiver and answered her questions. When the system told her to check a rapid diagnostic test for malaria, my colleague told her to assume the result was positive. She then took off her backpack and carefully set out its contents one by one: a scale for babies, a rapid test for malaria, and pulse oximeter. The fourth item she set down was the medication we were looking for, a treatment for malaria.

I wanted to know what she would do if she ran out of malaria tests or medications, a common scenario in her part of the world. She showed us how she would report the stock outage to her district manager using the mobile app. She then walked us through how she would modify her diagnostic protocol: If there weren't enough tests, she would diagnose malaria based on symptoms alone. If she didn't have enough medications, she would accompany the child to the nearest health post. Having the flexibility to modify her protocol was particularly valuable during the recent cyclones, which broke many of the country's supply chains.

On the long, bumpy drive back to the hotel, I recognized the wisdom of putting the ultimate responsibility of care for this village not in the Ministry of Health (three hours away by plane) or even in the district manager's office (an hour away by car) but in Ashanti's hands. Here, in one of the more remote corners of

Africa, we had a system of care that in many respects was more advanced than the one we have in the United States.

○—○—○

This final section is about the shift to *decentralized care*, which we define as shifting power—including responsibility, resources, and decision-making—from central governments and managed care organizations to public health authorities and employers, health workers, and, ultimately, patients.

Often when policymakers talk about decentralization, they are referring to shifting power from a national government to a subnational one. But what the Mozambiquan story shows is that the decentralization we need is much broader than that—it's about shifting responsibility, resources, and decision-making to the front lines of care. To do this, we need to empower individuals and organizations at the front lines, including patients and caregivers, with the tools and the resources to organize care in the ways that make most sense for their communities.

It's worth noting the difference between the terms *decentralized* and *distributed*. Although they commonly coexist, as in the example of Ashanti, they are not the same. Distributed, covered in Part I, refers to where care happens, whereas decentralized refers to who delivers care and how decisions are made. In Mozambique, care could be delivered in the community (distributed) but only provided by doctors and nurses (not decentralized). Conversely, care could be delivered in clinics (not distributed), but healthcare workers in those facilities could be given the resources to proactively engage households who needed care (decentralized).

During Covid-19 we saw the benefits of this shift. As policymakers relaxed restrictions on payment for telemedicine, doctors practicing across state lines, and communication over FaceTime and messaging, frontline health workers were able to pivot to virtual care, which created a lifeline for patients needing testing for Covid-19.[3] But limitations of a narrow approach to decentralization became evident as well. The rigid payment model of primary care made it impossible for clinics to deploy doctors to patients' homes or provide transportation to patients with the greatest needs. As a result, preventive and chronic care suffered. The same forms of decentralization that enabled Ashanti to respond to the cyclone that hit Mozambique could have made our system more resilient against Covid-19.

In Chapter 9, we discuss the need to put more resources, responsibility, and decision-making in the hands of front-line health workers. In Chapter 10, we discuss the ultimate in decentralization—transferring power to patients—which I call patient-directed.

CHAPTER 9

FRONT LINES
FIRST

PUTTING CARE IN THE
HANDS OF DOCTORS
AND HEALTH WORKERS

Most people think of doctors and healthcare professionals as very autonomous, highly trained, and deeply
trusted professionals who can do whatever they think
is right for their patients. It may come as a surprise to hear that,
often, decisions about healthcare aren't in the hands of doctors
today. Although we are largely in charge of making a diagnosis or deciding what medications to prescribe, when it comes to
how healthcare is delivered—which patients we see, what services we provide, and how patients receive them—we have little
agency.

That's because healthcare is still highly centralized. In the
United States, insurance companies and government payers
effectively tell us what healthcare services we can and cannot

provide by specifying what they will pay for. In the predominant fee-for-service model, what's paid for is what's provided.

I remember fondly a former patient of mine, a sweet woman in her mid-60s, who had been in and out of the hospital multiple times for heart failure. After one of her hospital stays, I reminded her to check her weight every day, and if her weight was up by two or three pounds—an early sign of impending heart failure—to call me.

As soon as I stepped out of the room, it occurred to me that she might not even have a scale. I went back in, sat down beside her, and asked, "Do you have a scale at home?" She was embarrassed to admit she didn't. She wanted one but just couldn't afford it. I checked the supply closet to see if we had a spare. We didn't, so I went back into the exam room and handed her a $20 bill from my wallet. She bought herself a simple bathroom scale the next day and hasn't been hospitalized since.

Centralization in healthcare isn't just a conceptual flaw with how healthcare is designed. It's a real problem that has real consequences on the front lines of care every day. It means that I can admit my patient to the hospital and rack up a $10,000 bill, but I can't get her a $20 scale so she doesn't need to be hospitalized in the first place. This frustrating situation is rooted in the fact that, in healthcare, responsibility is somewhat synonymous with risk. When a patient gets sick, who bears the cost? When a patient is not their healthiest, who is responsible?

Historically in the United States, this risk has been borne by insurance companies and the government through Medicare and Medicaid. If someone with kidney disease is admitted to the hospital, the insurer pays. If that person is then discharged by the hospital and readmitted, the insurer pays again. Hospitals and doctors do not bear the risk. In fact, somewhat perversely, the sicker a patient gets, the more hospitals and doctors get paid. Although patients with insurance certainly suffer a great cost in terms of health and well-being, and sometimes get stuck with absurdly high bills, they do not bear the financial risk—their insurers do.

In a recent conversation, Rahul Rajkumar, a friend and chief medical officer of Blue Cross Blue Shield of North Carolina, put it more simply, "We pay for healthcare by the yard."

Rahul, a Yale-educated physician executive, has dedicated his career to making healthcare better and more affordable by changing how we pay for care. His aha moment came early in his career on a visit to his grandparents in India. Right before Rahul's eyes, his grandfather had a stroke and Rahul managed to get him to the hospital within the narrow window of time needed to administer lifesaving treatment. But shockingly, the doctors there refused to treat him until they were paid first—in cash. "I realized that the practice of medicine is shaped by the way we finance it. The way we pay for it signals what we value."

What we should value, Rahul argues, is efficiency and excellence in the delivery of healthcare. The ultimate goal, as he sees it, is for doctors to be accountable for the total cost of care and decide how to provide care in the most effective and efficient way possible. And that may be through capitation—paying doctors for the patients they care for instead of each individual service they provide—or by building accountable care organizations (ACOs) that give providers a right-sized amount of risk. He notes that had we had such a system during the pandemic, many primary care doctors' offices, which shut down as they saw their revenues decline by up to 50 percent, would have remained open.

But the problems of centralization go beyond payment. Healthcare is also highly regulated. Doctors and other healthcare professionals have a dizzying number of limitations on what we can do. I can't see my patients by video or phone (except during a pandemic). My nurses can't draw patients' blood at home. My clinic can't see a patient for a physical health appointment and a mental health appointment on the same day. The list goes on and on. As far as I know, I may have broken some sort of rule by giving my patient money to buy a scale![1]

The intent of many of these regulations is good. Policymakers are well-intentioned and hardworking people who want to do the right thing, and their charge is an essential one: upholding the safety and quality of healthcare, protecting patients and the general public from fraud and abuse, and managing overall healthcare costs.

So what is the way forward? How do we thread the needle between giving healthcare workers greater autonomy and control while ensuring the safety, quality, and cost-effectiveness of care?

A VISION OF FRONT LINES FIRST

The vision of front lines first is simply that—we put the front lines first. Any effort to improve healthcare quality, to drive greater accountability for health outcomes, or to improve population health, starts by putting more responsibility, resources, and decision-making in the hands of frontline care teams.

Many healthcare insiders will immediately recognize that many of the ideas I'm discussing here relate to population health or value-based care. When people in healthcare think of "population health" they think big—insurance companies, managed care organizations, and health systems with millions of patients. The general public thinks even bigger. Population health is often considered synonymous with "public health," which conjures up images of the Centers for Disease Control and Prevention and the World Health Organization.

But to me, population health starts small. It begins with recognizing that, ultimately, population health is practiced one patient at a time.

When I worked at a large population health company early in my career, I saw that too often population health and value-based care were about what happened outside of a doctor's visit. They were about new payment schemes, new contracting models, and new billing practices. Often, the doctors and nurses had no idea that their health systems had taken on greater risk for the very patients they were taking care of. The people with the greatest responsibility for patient care were left out!

To me, the clearest vision of where we need to go is an image etched in my mind: Ashanti, in her bright green uniform, going from household to household, checking up on her patients and dispensing treatments—in effect, providing "population health" for an entire village.

When I contrast how I deliver care in Washington, DC, to how Ashanti does in rural Mozambique, I'm stunned to realize how many more tools she has than I do. Front lines first envisions that doctors and other healthcare workers will be empowered in ways they aren't today. I articulate a number of them as follows.

We Will Know Who We Are Responsible For

What struck me most about Ashanti is that she feels deeply accountable for the health and well-being of an entire population. It's no accident that in explaining her work, the first thing she did was draw a map. She knows exactly who her patients are and who she is responsible for.

If you walked into my clinic and asked me the question I asked her, "How do you know what patients to see?" I'd pull up my appointment schedule for the day and say, "These are the patients I need to see."

But that's a very different thing. It means that I'm seeing only the patients who schedule appointments with me and who can make it to clinic for their appointments. But those may not be the patients who need me most. In fact, in my experience, they often aren't. It's the patient who hasn't seen a doctor in 10 years and has a ticking time bomb in his chest or the patient who misses most of her appointments because of crippling depression who actually need care the most and whom our healthcare system most often fails.

What's more, if you asked me to show you my population, I wouldn't be able to. My electronic health record is designed around individual patient visits—a by-product of the way our healthcare system pays for care—not populations. There is no tab that lists all of my patients. Even when I ask one of my clinic's data analysts to manually create such a list for me, it's not what Ashanti has. What I receive is a list of patients who have seen me in the past 12 months. What I really want to know is who are all of the patients who are assigned to me—those I see regularly as well as those I've never seen before. Doing this would require my clinic to decide who we are responsible for—which neighborhoods, what households, which patients are ours. In effect, we'd need to start by drawing a map.

We Will Know Who Needs Our Help

Ashanti knows exactly not only who her patients are but also who needs help most. On her mobile app, she has a task list that guides her on which households to visit each day and what health checks to perform.

Her task list is an example of a simple but brilliant solution to a very hard problem. How do you use data to help healthcare workers proactively manage a population? Although her task list appears to be little more than a standard shopping list, under the hood, it is based on advanced algorithms that combine multiple sources of data: geocoded location data, demographic and health data, and evidence-based clinical protocols. The list she pulled up on her phone was a solution to the kind of complex math problem that would take an MIT engineer to figure out.

And in fact, it was. I know, because the developer of the software, Jonathan Jackson, the founder and CEO of Dimagi, was a classmate of mine at MIT. Jonathan is also brilliant enough to know that data isn't enough—that it's one thing to have a lot of data, but it's quite another to have that data be actionable. That's what Jonathan was aiming for when he designed an app so user-friendly that the only thing the APE sees is a suggested list of households to visit and tasks to perform.[2]

We Will Know How We Are Performing

Ashanti also knows on an individual level how she is doing. She isn't simply charged with completing tasks; she's responsible for results. That spells the difference between accountability and micromanagement.

At a local level, she tracks key outcomes of care—like childhood and maternal deaths—and each month she meets to review them with her supervisor, so she is aware of where she stands relative to the goals set by her community and the ministry of health.

Most critical for her are the set of indicators she is responsible for—factors tied to health outcomes that are within her control, like the percentage of women who have four or more prenatal visits or who have delivered in a hospital. She can see her performance on these indicators compared to her goals within her mobile phone application. These indicators are crucial because they drive accountability. Simply visiting the household of a pregnant woman and checking the box in her task list isn't enough. Ashanti's responsible for making it possible for the woman to deliver her baby in a hospital where the risk of complications is lower.

In my clinic we don't routinely track health outcomes and don't have clear quality goals. Deaths that occur in a hospital or at home are recorded on a different electronic system than the one my clinic uses. If we hear about a death, it's often by chance, passed along in hushed hallway conversations. We look at quality, but primarily on the individual visit level. I'm peer-reviewed by my colleagues based on my charts, which is largely an exercise in how well I document rather than how well I practice medicine. And other leading indicators, like the percentage of my patients with diabetes who have their blood sugar controlled or have seen me at least twice in the past year, are either unavailable or not routinely reported.

We Will Have the Resources and Autonomy to Succeed

Another key lesson I learned from Mozambique is that it's not enough to make doctors and healthcare workers accountable for population health. We also must give them the resources and autonomy to succeed.

In the United States there is a growing movement toward accountable care—new arrangements between insurance companies and health systems that financially reward doctors for improving health outcomes and lowering costs. As in Mozambique, these arrangements often start by first identifying the population that the doctors are accountable for and then defining the measures of success. But many of these accountable care organizations (or ACOs) have had limited results.[3] One of the core problems is that while responsibility has shifted to doctors and other healthcare workers, decision-making authority and resources have not.

In contrast, Ashanti has both. In her backpack the day I met her, she had a thermometer, pulse oximeter, rapid diagnostic tests, wound care kits, antibiotics, and rehydration treatments—a mini-clinic of sorts. She also has the authority to use them. Despite having considerably fewer years of education and training, she is able to do far more than my nurses are allowed to do.

Her power extends beyond what's in her backpack. If Ashanti identifies a household without proper sanitation, she can notify the village leaders, who in turn will send laborers to install a toilet system. This can reduce the risk of childhood diarrhea (a common cause of death in children under age five in many low- and middle-income countries). In effect, the interventions available to her as a healthcare worker can address not only biomedical needs but also social and environmental ones—something our system in the United States struggles with and is core to population health.

She is also empowered to make her own decisions. The tasks she receives each day on her list are suggestions. Ultimately, she decides which households to see. If, in passing one household on her way to another, she learns that they have a sick child, it makes sense for her to attend to that patient. But imagine instead that the central government had decided that community health workers could only visit households on their task list; she would miss the sick child. Such a scenario may seem absurd, but in fact, it's exactly how healthcare in the United States typically works.

Ashanti also has flexibility to respond to what she is seeing on the ground. The shortages of testing we were shocked to see in the United States during Covid-19 is a common occurrence in many parts of the world like Mozambique. If Ashanti sees that her supply is getting low, she is able to adjust her protocols on the fly. This proved essential when the cyclone hit. It made the entire healthcare system resilient and agile. It was able to move care to where it was needed most, rather than being stuck in the sand—something that we in the United States are now all too familiar with.

REALIZING THE VISION

What will it take to empower frontline health workers at scale? Realizing this vision will require multiple shifts.

Giving Frontline Health Workers the Resources They Need

The first step is paying doctors differently. When primary care physicians—already operating with razor-thin margins—are paid per visit or per procedure, they can't invest in the kinds of services and tools they believe are needed to serve their patients, like transportation vouchers or home-based care. Instead, we need to give primary care physicians a fixed amount of money per month or per year to take care of their patients. The second step is to give doctors, nurses, and frontline care teams a voice in how those resources are allocated. If the clinic is paid a fixed fee each month, but administrators still direct how those resources are spent, it's not much different than a health plan having control of those resources. The administrator can't foresee how a $20 scale might spare a patient a trip to the hospital, but her doctor can.

Perhaps the best-known examples of this happening effectively in the United States are risk-based or value-based primary care clinics like Oak Street Health, Iora Health, and ChenMed. In these models, primary care doctors get a fixed amount of money to manage all of their patients' healthcare needs. No matter how many patient visits, how many diagnostic tests, and how many hospitalizations, doctors get paid the same amount—one that is predetermined depending on the overall health of each patient and is paid to them unless they don't meet certain quality and outcome measures.

With these resources, these clinics have been built from the ground up to better meet the needs of their patients. For example, rather than locating clinics in a medical building or hospital well out of the way for their patients and with impossible parking, they place them in high-traffic retail spaces in the neighborhood, making it easy for patients to drop by. Oak Street Health and ChenMed make it even more convenient by putting a pharmacy in the clinic, which they've found also increases medication adherence.[4]

Risk-based primary care practices also have the resources to hire health workers who typically aren't reimbursed by insurance companies. At Iora, when patients walk into the clinic, they are paired with a dedicated health coach who prepares them for the visit with the doctor, participates in the visit, and then follows up with them afterward to help them stick with their care plan.[5] They also pay for services that many clinics couldn't even dream of affording, such as door-to-door transportation—a barrier for many patients, particularly the elderly and individuals with mobility issues. During Covid-19, Oak Street Health went even further by transforming its fleet of mobile vans to deliver groceries, household and medical supplies, and medications to people's homes.

The model also allows clinics to move outside the traditional biomedical model of care. ChenMed has a community space for free tai chi and yoga classes. They also host monthly birthday parties to reduce social isolation, a significant risk factor for both mental and physical health issues.[6]

My friend Ali Khan, a physician at Oak Street Health, gave me an example from Covid-19 that illustrates why this model is so powerful. He told me about a patient on the West Side of Chicago who for years had uncontrolled diabetes, but who had achieved her lowest blood sugar levels in years during the pandemic, thanks to the ability of Oak Street to adapt care to her needs. When Ali called to congratulate her, she responded, "I did the work, but you guys kept me going. I had people helping me adjust my sugars. I had people bringing me food—even toilet paper. When I called on the phone, you answered. Yes, I did the work, but you kept me on the right path."

Giving Frontline Health Workers Time and Space

Changing healthcare is about changing clinical workflows—the sequence of tasks and routine of a healthcare worker's day. As many doctors say, "If it's not in my clinical workflow, it's not going to happen." But much of healthcare is organized around individual patient visits. How can we insert population health into a clinical workflow that is largely filled with visit after visit?

A simple framework I've found helpful is to figure out what decisions frontline health workers need to make each day, each week, and each month, and then get them just the right information they need to make decisions in those moments.

Each morning, I want to know who is coming in for care that day and what care they need. I also want to know who needs to be seen urgently who isn't already on the schedule. Daily huddles are highly effective for managing this. With huddles, instead of jumping right into my first visit of the day, I take a few minutes to sit down with my medical assistant to review all the patients we'll see that day. Together, we flag patients who need a flu shot or a foot exam for diabetes and make a plan to ensure those things happen—for example, by ordering the flu shot ahead of time so my medical assistant can give it while I'm wrapping up with another patient or by removing a patient's shoes when they arrive for their appointment. Huddles also give us an opportunity to discuss any urgent communications from patients who need a call back or who were just discharged from the hospital, so we can make time in the day to reach out to them.

Each week, I want to know that the patients I saw that week are getting the appropriate follow-up and care. Did my patient with high blood pressure actually start his new medication? Was the urgent appointment with the cardiologist scheduled? I also want an opportunity to consult with colleagues on my more complicated patients. Through weekly case rounds over lunch, I can discuss these cases with a multidisciplinary team of doctors, nurses, and social workers and develop a comprehensive plan to help them.

Each month, I want to ensure that I'm actively caring for patients with complex medical needs and improving the health of my population. To do so, I need a list of my highest-risk patients and objective measures of how close I'm coming to meeting the goals I set for them. Through a monthly panel review, I can review my data with my medical director and nurse and figure out what changes we need to make to our overall practice.

Giving Frontline Health Workers Data They Can Use

Frontline health workers need data and analytics tools that help them sort patients based on risk levels and identify which ones need care—a task list like Ashanti's. Despite millions of dollars of investment in our electronic health record, it is little more than a scanned version of a paper chart. It is far less sophisticated than what Ashanti has. For example, I can't query it for a list of patients with diabetes who have not had a recent visit with me. With such a list, I could ensure I was reaching everyone who needed help and call those who I hadn't seen in a while. And this query is very basic. Ideally, these analytics tools would be running much more sophisticated algorithms using machine learning to predict which patients are at greatest risk of preventable complications.

Regardless of how sophisticated these tools are, they must be usable and actionable. I remember years ago when I worked at Evolent Health, a population health company, a brilliant data scientist excitedly grabbing me in the hallway to show me a medication report she had developed. With impressive graphic displays and filtering capabilities, it showed a doctor's monthly pharmacy spend compared to their peers. The sample data showed a doctor who spent $X per patient per month on medications compared to an average of $Y per patient per month. But when I asked her what she expected doctors to do with that information, she wasn't sure, "Think about spending less on medications, I guess." But then she noted that many patients appeared to be taking two drugs of the same class of medications—like two statin cholesterol-lowering drugs—a costly and also potentially dangerous situation. Together, we modified the report to show doctors a list of all of their patients on duplicate medications. Now the data was actionable. Doctors could quickly scan and check off which medications patients should be on and then hand the list off to a nurse to help patients get on the right medication.

Giving Frontline Health Workers Greater Autonomy

In healthcare, we often talk about the need to help healthcare workers operate at the "top of their license," but if we want to dramatically expand access to care while lowering cost, we need to help them operate at the top of the *next* license. A case example is Ashanti, who despite having less than a high school education, is diagnosing malaria on her own with the help of software and rapid diagnostic tests.

Today, in my practice, even though more and more of our care is team-based, I still retain much of the authority. My nurse can see patients for blood pressure checks, but only I can adjust the dosage of their blood pressure medications. My medical assistant can call my patients with their lab results, but only I can counsel my patients on what they mean.

These policies overwhelm doctors with tasks that could be delegated to other care team members, which contributes to physician burnout and limits the professional growth of nurses and nonphysician healthcare professionals. To address this, we will need a sea change in how we think about accreditation, licensing, and scope of practice.

Transforming Frontline Health Workers into Leaders

Shifting care from a reactionary, fee-for-service model to a proactive, population health model isn't just about tools and staff. It requires a complete overhaul in how doctors and care teams practice medicine. When I worked at Evolent Health, we recognized that ultimately this change was about leadership. We created a training program called LEAP, or Leadership Education Applied to Practice, that gave clinicians hands-on training in this new model of care. One of the keys to the program's success was that we didn't just train the physicians—we'd also invite a nurse and an operations leader—but also made the training practical by giving them reports based on actual data from their practices and coaching them to design and implement quality improvement projects.

STRATEGIC ACTIONS

The shift to decentralized care will create new opportunities to empower healthcare workers to take charge of the populations they serve. Doing so successfully will require not only shifting risks but also resources and decision-making to these providers, so that those closest to care can decide who receives it and how and what is delivered. This will require new kinds of expertise, training in population health, and a culture of accountability.

Although many of the examples in this chapter are of healthcare organizations, most of the same principles and ideas apply to other settings that employ frontline care teams, such as health plans, employers, and public health departments.

Here are some steps that all of us can take to accelerate our path to putting the front lines first and position ourselves and our organizations to succeed.

Patients, Caregivers, and Consumers of Care

* Seek out doctors who practice in risk-bearing primary care clinics and accountable care organizations. A good question to ask is, "Do you get paid fee-for-service or do you get paid a fixed amount to address all of my healthcare needs?" If you are on Medicare, sign up for Medicare Advantage or an innovative Medicare Advantage clinic.

Physicians and Healthcare Professionals

* Work in hospitals and clinics that reward you for better patient outcomes, and emphasize prevention and patient well-being, such as risk-bearing primary care clinics and accountable care organizations.

- Invest five minutes every morning to huddle with your care team—the Institute for Healthcare Improvement has great resources for getting started—and 15 minutes each week to proactively track and follow up on patients you worry about the most.

Healthcare Delivery Systems, Including Traditional and Technology Enabled

- Define the population you are accountable for ("draw the map"), and establish success measures for your full population, not just those who engage in care.

- Ensure every patient knows who their doctor is and every doctor knows who their patients are.

- Build a management structure that cascades communication from administrators down to frontline health workers. If your frontline care teams don't know about or understand a new payment model or quality improvement initiative, it won't work.

- Seek out opportunities to take on greater risk of your populations, from pay-for-performance and upside risk opportunities to bundled payments and risk-based capitation.

- Invest in services like transportation and care models like mobile clinics to reach more of your population, especially your most vulnerable patients.

Employers

- Demand that health plans and vendors share data not only on utilization but also on outcomes. In return, share your claims data and data on employee benefits with vendors to empower their healthcare workers.

- Invest in population health services—including proactive identification and outreach, care navigation, and disease management—that are proven to improve health outcomes and costs.

- Consolidate your vendor relationships through one partner—if you're large enough, through one internal management structure—that can ensure appropriate utilization, drive accountability, and report on population-level engagement and outcomes.

- Build your organizational capacity to manage population health. Hire a chief medical officer or set up a medical advisory board, and then empower them to make major decisions that impact your business.

Health Plans and Government Payers

- Reimburse new models of care—such as telehealth (particularly for primary care and mental health), mobile health, and hospital-at-home—that give doctors more options for best managing the health of their patients.

- Accelerate your path to risk sharing and risk-based capitation.

- Invest in data sharing and reporting at the individual provider level to empower frontline health workers with data.

- Be willing to pay providers upfront so they can invest in new capabilities and infrastructure required to successfully manage risk.

Policymakers

- Reduce the administrative burden on providers by simplifying and consolidating quality measures.

- Enable multipayer arrangements to strengthen the business case for providers to invest in population health.

- Remove obstacles to delivery system innovation. Don't regulate specific services. Instead, hold providers accountable for results.

- Enable team-based care and upskilling by relaxing restrictions on what nonphysician healthcare professionals can do.

Healthcare Investors and Entrepreneurs

Invest in and build companies that:

- Enable accurate patient attribution (assigning patients to specific doctors and practices).

- Create prioritized task lists for providers based on patient needs.

- Delegate or automate tasks that do not require a doctor's or nurse's expertise.

- Predict impact, not just future costs.

- Enable multichannel proactive outreach.

CHAPTER 10

PATIENT-DIRECTED

EMPOWERING PEOPLE TO GUIDE THEIR OWN CARE

When I was a third-year medical student rotating through the hospital, I kept seeing patient after patient suffer from health problems that were completely preventable: a high-risk woman in her fifties who had a heart attack, but wasn't taking a preventive dose of aspirin every day; an elderly man with colon cancer who had never had colon cancer screening; a mother of three who missed her flu shot and wound up in the ICU with pneumonia.

As I encountered these patients, I'd call my mother and relay the missed recommendations to her one by one. She was in her fifties with type 2 diabetes, and at a stage in her life when health was less of a given and more of a concern.

She went from welcoming my suggestions to feeling overwhelmed by them. At one point out of frustration, she said,

"Can't you just give me *one* list of everything I need to do?" So I did. I sat down, reviewed all the medical literature on preventive health I could get my hands on, and came up with all of the evidence-based preventive healthcare measures she needed. To make it feel more manageable, I handed it to her in the form of a checklist, like one she'd take to the grocery store.

While the medicine and science behind preventive healthcare is complex, the recommendations are straightforward. In fact, if you know your age and your gender, you know 90 percent of the preventive measures you need. If you're an adult, you need a tetanus shot every 10 years. If you're 50 and a woman, you need regular mammograms.

So I decided to build checklists for every decade of life and publish them in a book, which I wrote during my final year of medical school. At the beginning of *Stay Healthy at Every Age* were the checklists by age, followed by chapters on each item in the checklist. Readers could find the checklist for them and then turn to the chapters for the items on their list.

After the book came out during my medical residency, I put the checklists online for anyone to access for free. With a friend of mine, Gaurav Singal, I built a simple website where patients could enter their demographic and basic health information and receive a personalized checklist to print out and take to the doctor's office.

I was curious whether the checklists were actually useful to people. Together with some medical students at the University of Chicago, I designed a research study and conducted user interviews with individuals we recruited from the community. We observed participants using the website and asked them detailed questions about it afterward. The results were encouraging. Ninety-six percent found it easy to use and 64 percent reported learning something new.[1]

However, when we followed up with them later, it seemed like the website had less impact on their actual care than we had hoped. Many users had no doctor at all or had difficulty going in to see one. Some simply wanted to get the recommended services on their own but learned that they couldn't just walk into an imaging center for a mammogram or go to a lab testing center and ask for a blood test for diabetes—they needed a doctor's order. Others had a doctor, but didn't feel empowered to voice their concerns at the visit. Still others wanted to make the lifestyle changes recommended in the checklists—like quitting smoking or losing weight—but struggled to find resources to help them. Finally, there were the patients—particularly those who lived paycheck to paycheck and juggled childcare, senior care, and work responsibilities—who felt that the information was overwhelming. They needed someone to help them manage it.

My checklists were a step in the right direction. But if I wanted to truly solve the problem that I encountered in the hospital, I'd need to do much more than give people the right health information. As my engineering friends would say, information was necessary but not sufficient. And yet, as I've navigated the healthcare industry and the health-tech world, I've observed that providing patients access to better information is by and large what many see as the whole solution to healthcare.

In this chapter I discuss the shift to patient-directed care—a world where patients provide more of their own care and guide more of their healthcare decisions. As I learned from my checklist example, *patient-directed care* is as much about transferring responsibility, resources, and decision-making to patients as it is about making the system simpler for patients to access and use on their own.

I purposely use the term *patient-directed* over the more common industry term *consumer-directed* for two reasons. For one, the term *consumer-directed* is often associated with a largely failed experiment in the 1990s, in which patients were given more responsibility to pay for healthcare services—what proponents called "skin in the game"—along with software tools to help them make better decisions. The other is that I don't consider patients to be consumers in the traditional sense. Unlike consumers, patients often don't know how to assess the quality of healthcare services and make tradeoffs between price and quality. Moreover, when you are acutely ill, it's difficult to impossible to shop for care—you just want a system that works.

VISION OF PATIENT-DIRECTED CARE

It may seem as though care is patient-directed today; after all, it's usually patients who get the ball rolling by calling their doctors when they have symptoms or health concerns. But once they initiate the process, they may find themselves swept into a system that doesn't work as well as it could for them—and that is anything but patient-directed. The following hypothetical example illustrates the point.

How Care Works Today

Imagine that a close friend was just diagnosed with type 2 diabetes. Your friend mentions that her doctor thinks she might have had type 2 diabetes for years and wasn't aware of it. By leaving her diabetes untreated, she may have caused preventable damage to her body. Her diagnosis shakes you. Although you have been meaning to, you haven't seen a primary care doctor in years. So you decide to get checked out.

Your first step is to find a doctor. You dig out your health insurance card. After multiple tries and password resets, you manage to log onto your health insurance portal and find a list of doctors who take your insurance. You call several doctors' offices, wending your way through interactive voice menus and waiting on hold for long stretches. After more than 30 minutes you reach someone only to find out that the doctor isn't taking new patients. Finally, on your fifth attempt, you find a doctor who is accepting new patients. You ask for the first available appointment. The earliest slot is three weeks away. You grab it.

On the appointed day, after requesting a half-day off work, you arrive at the flagship hospital of a large system and nearly miss your appointment trying to find parking. You wait in the reception area, completing a bunch of paperwork on your medical history and symptoms and then idling on your phone. Nearly 45 minutes after your scheduled appointment time, a nurse calls your name. You feel like you've won the lottery! The nurse checks your blood pressure and your weight. She asks you a lot of the same questions you've just answered on the waiting-room forms, but this time she is entering the information into a computer. When she finishes that task, she takes you to the exam room. Finally, an hour after your scheduled appointment time, the doctor arrives.

He seems nice. He asks you what brings you into the clinic. About 20 seconds into your story about your friend, he interrupts. He tells you how important it is that you see the doctor regularly. He's going to order blood work and let you know if any of the results are abnormal. He then checks your pulse and places his stethoscope over your heart and lungs while he continues talking. You manage to get a word in edgewise, asking if one of the blood tests will be for diabetes. He says, "Yes, absolutely." You then get your blood drawn. You have spent two hours at the medical center. The total amount of time you spent with the doctor was five minutes.

Two days have passed since your appointment. You still haven't heard back from the doctor. You download the clinic's patient app. After multiple tries and calls to the doctor's office, you log in and pull up your blood test results. You don't recognize many of the tests, so you google them one by one, until you get to a term that says *hemoglobin A1c*—a test that you learn measures the average glucose levels in the blood over the last three months.

Yours is 6.4 percent. A level below 5.7 is considered normal, 5.7 percent to 6.4 percent indicates prediabetes, and 6.5 percent and higher indicates diabetes. With an A1c value of 6.4 percent, you have prediabetes.

You read what you can about prediabetes and wait a couple more days for the doctor's call. It doesn't come. Finally, you call the clinic. After a long wait time, someone lets you know that the doctor will call you back. A day later, the doctor calls you. He tells you that you indeed have prediabetes. You need to lose weight. He instructs you to come back in three months to have your A1c level rechecked.

For the next two weeks, you're motivated. You make a number of changes—you cut out junk food and exercise more. You even feel like you've lost a pound or two. You have no way of knowing what your blood sugars are, but your doctor told you to focus on your weight. Then things get busier at work and at home and your plans get lost in the mix. Three months have flown by before you realize that it's time for your appointment. After the same rigmarole, you get to see the doctor for a few minutes. He admonishes you for not losing weight. He checks your blood sugar again. This time it's above the limit. You have type 2 diabetes.

Many of us have had an experience like this. It's frustrating. It's dehumanizing. But it doesn't have to be that way. In this example, you had insurance, you had a doctor, and you even caught your prediabetes early, yet you developed diabetes anyway. This isn't just an isolated example. There are over 88 million adults in the United States with prediabetes[2] and many more with other conditions that are entirely preventable or treatable, and yet we fail to do so.

How Care Could Work

Now we are going to walk through an alternative version of this example—a vision of what is possible. Suppose a friend of yours was recently diagnosed with type 2 diabetes and you decide to get checked out. You open your health app to message your concern or call a health line. A healthcare professional directs you to complete a standardized assessment. After a couple minutes, you've provided your weight, height, family history, and medical history. The assessment you completed may be reviewed by a doctor who makes a recommendation on next steps, but in your case, it is algorithmically scored by software, and the system is able to automatically recommend that you get tested for type 2 diabetes. You are given the option of testing yourself at home—by picking up a test kit or having one mailed to you—or getting tested at a nearby laboratory.

Feeling unsure about pricking your own finger, you choose the lab option. A lab slip is instantly sent to your phone. You are able to get tested as soon as you like—no appointment is required. An hour later you drive to the lab testing center, and within a couple minutes you've gotten your blood drawn.

The next day you get a notification that your results are available. You check the phone app and see your results graphically displayed in a way that helps you understand your risk of diabetes. Using the app, you open up a video about prediabetes and how you can manage it.

The app also recommends that you see a doctor. You are given the option to set up a virtual visit or an in-person visit. With a young family at home and a busy job, you choose the former. Since you don't have a doctor currently, you are given a list of doctors to choose from. Each doctor's listing includes the types of patients they most commonly see, their performance on various quality measures, and a brief blurb about why they went into medicine and their hobbies and interests.

You choose a doctor who seems like a great fit for you and schedule an appointment for later that day. Sitting in the comfort of your own home, and with your spouse joining in from your daughter's softball game, you start the video call. The doctor is sitting in an office with her medical degrees visible on the wall behind her and has a kind demeanor. She starts by introducing herself as your new primary care doctor and getting to know you. She's already reviewed the initial intake form and your lab results. She helps you understand that your elevated blood sugar is really a warning sign—and an opportunity. Years ago, people had no way of knowing they were at risk for diabetes until they came to the doctor at an advanced stage. She commends you for catching it early and tells you that by losing five to seven pounds, you could prevent yourself from getting diabetes. Although you knew much of this information already from the videos you watched, it's comforting to hear it from a doctor and the reinforcement is helpful. You and your spouse feel listened to and far from alone as you grapple with your new condition.

She recommends enrolling in a weight-loss and diabetes prevention program to help you stay on track until your next appointment in six weeks. There are a few options. The first is a digital app supported by virtual coaches. The second is a group class at a nearby community center that is accredited by the CDC. The third is a one-on-one, in-home program, but the price is out of your budget. You prefer an in-person experience so you choose the second option. The system indicates in real time that it's fully covered by your insurance.

Your follow-up visit with your doctor is six weeks later. Two days beforehand you receive an app notification asking you to repeat your blood work. This time you choose to do the test at home. You pick up the kit—which contains a lancet, blood collecting device, and a monitor—from the pharmacy. Once you're home, you prick your finger, collect the blood sample, and insert it into the monitor. The monitor displays the result five minutes later. You take a photo of the result and upload it to your health app. It displays the result—6.1 percent—and compares it to your last reading. There are links to additional reading materials.

On your next video visit with the doctor, she starts by congratulating you. Your blood sugar is down. You're well on your way to preventing type 2 diabetes! Your doctor uses the rest of the visit to help you catch up on other preventive care that you're due for—cancer screenings, blood pressure measurement, and vaccinations that can help you stay as healthy as possible.

o—o—o

What makes this version of the story feel so different from the first is that you, the patient, were in control at every step. You knew your options and understood the pros and cons and the price of each; you had the knowledge and skills to take action and make behavior changes; you were able to access the system when and where you needed it, on your own terms. Put another way, you happened to care; care didn't just happen to you. The result was that you prevented type 2 diabetes from developing.

We have all the components to make this vision a reality today. There are dozens of similar health apps, freestanding lab-testing centers in nearly every county in the country, a growing number of telemedicine services that provide not just urgent care but also primary care services, a national diabetes prevention program through the YMCA that is proven to work and is covered by insurance companies, and at-home diabetes test kits that are FDA-approved and commercially available to patients. What's missing is a system of care that stitches all of the pieces together and makes it widely available to everyone.

MODELS OF PATIENT-DIRECTED CARE

The vision I described integrates a number of care models that I've discussed previously, including virtual primary care (Chapter 2) and advocacy services (Chapter 4). It also includes three new models that I will cover here—facilitated self-service, at-home self-testing, and self-management training.

Facilitated Self-Service

Self-service—customers purchasing products and services without an intermediary—is becoming the dominant transaction model in the United States and other parts of the world. It's increasingly how we shop, get our groceries, and pay our taxes.

As defined by David Asch, a physician and researcher at the University of Pennsylvania, and colleagues in a paper published in *The New England Journal of Medicine*, "Facilitated self-service means consumers can handle most of their needs without help, but some needs require a higher level of service. Most travel arrangements are easily made online, but occasionally you need to call the airline. Your tax-preparation software does nearly everything, but some questions require the online-chat feature or, in a real jam, an accountant."[3]

In some cases, facilitated self-service in medicine will mean care can be accessed without a doctor at all, just like over-the-counter medications and pregnancy tests. In other cases, patients will be able to request these services and have their request immediately reviewed by a doctor without being seen. We saw such self-service models during the Covid-19 pandemic. Patients were able to complete a self-assessment online or in person that asked: Do you have a fever? Do you have a cough? Have you been exposed to anyone with Covid-19? This information was then reviewed behind-the-scenes by a physician, often within minutes, who either signed off on the order for a Covid-19 test or decided that a medical appointment was required first.

The critical difference with how healthcare works today is that care can start without the doctor. That means that the physician-patient encounter, which Dr. Asch refers to as "healthcare's choke point," is eliminated completely, or at least pushed to a later step in the process when it's more needed. And this choke point is real, particularly for many of the patients who need it most, including people living in poverty, rural communities, and racial and ethnic minorities, who struggle with getting medical appointments.

Facilitated self-service is already coming to healthcare. Today, patients can get on birth control pills, quit smoking with the use of medications, and diagnose urinary tract infections—all from an app, without seeing a doctor.

The most obvious benefit of these services is convenience and access. Some offer to get prescriptions to women within two to three days by mail; others will have a prescription at a specified pharmacy within an hour. Contrast that to the experience of so many women who need to wait weeks for an appointment and spend an hour in the waiting room just to get a prescription for a birth control pill that they've been taking for years.

They also offer care at a cost that patients can afford—often as low as $15 to $20 for a visit and a month's supply of medication. I asked Ateev Mehrotra, a physician and expert in telemedicine at Harvard Medical School, how this was possible. He told me, "They can do it because one doctor can manage a thousand visits a day instead of the usual 30 or 40, because they only need to focus their energies on the five percent of patients who screen positive for contraindications. That allows them to radically drop the unit price of care."

At-Home Self-Testing

For years, patients with diabetes have been able to test their sugars at home by pricking their fingers, and women have been able to check their pregnancy status with a urine test. At-home test kits exist for a wide range of conditions from urinary tract infections to colon cancer screening to the flu and Covid-19. However, many of these tests aren't covered by insurance and aren't accepted by doctor's offices.

For me, this is deeply personal. My older daughter, Asha, was born with a congenital health condition that increases her risk of kidney infections. When she was a toddler, we had to get a urine test every time she had a fever to make sure it was just a common cold she picked up at daycare and not a kidney infection. This meant taking her to an urgent care center or emergency room—a scary place for a child—and worse, having a catheter placed into her bladder to get a clean urine sample. After putting her through this ordeal twice, my wife and I just couldn't do it anymore. Seeing the fear and pain in our child's eyes was too much to bear. Fortunately for us, as doctors, we had an alternative. My wife brought home a urine collection kit from her hospital, and the next time Asha had a fever, she was able to use it at home. But every family should have access to this. Healthcare shouldn't have to be so hard.

At-home testing also extends to biometric measurements. In the middle of the Covid-19 pandemic, my sister was told that her newborn baby's weight was too low and the pediatrician would need to see her baby more frequently to monitor it. My sister was distraught. Not only was she juggling a newborn baby and toddler at home while recovering from a C-section, she also had to worry about coming into a clinic and risking exposure to Covid-19.

A user-experience designer by trade, my sister soon came up with an alternative. She found a neighbor who had a baby scale she could borrow and then asked the clinic nurse to show her how to properly use it. As a result, she was able to do all of her follow-up visits virtually from home. What's more, instead of measuring the baby's weight every few days—and at different times of the day, depending on when her medical appointments were—she was able to weigh the baby at the same time each day, enabling her and her doctor to better track the baby's progress.

At-home testing also gave my sister a greater sense of control and ownership that comes from being able to do things for yourself. In her words, "I was worried whether I was doing enough to get my baby back on her growth curve. With the ability to weigh her myself, I not only had the comfort of knowing that she was doing OK but also it helped me decide whether I should squeeze in one more feed or supplement with formula."

Self-Management Support

In the alternate vision of the prediabetes situation I presented earlier, what ultimately prevented you from getting diabetes wasn't seeing a doctor or getting tested for diabetes. It was the diabetes prevention group class you signed up for.

The idea behind that intervention—what's known as self-management support—has its origins in a landmark study published in 1999 by Kate Lorig, a pioneering nurse-researcher at Stanford. Until her study was published, it was largely assumed that chronic diseases were too complex for many patients to manage on their own, and certainly too complex for nonmedical professionals to teach patients how to manage. However, as a Peace Corps volunteer in Chile, Lorig had seen health workers with little formal training effectively run the healthcare system. She drew upon that experience to design a class where individuals with chronic conditions taught their peers how to manage their own health. Rather than providing lectures, which is how doctors are largely trained, the peer leaders were taught to act more like coaches. They helped participants set weekly goals for themselves, modeled behaviors and problem solving, and assisted them in making choices. For example, rather than saying, "You should cut down on carbs," they asked, "What healthier food choices do you want to try this week?"

In her study, Lorig randomly assigned people with a range of chronic diseases to two groups. One group took a 150-minute class once a week for seven weeks; the other didn't. Lorig's team checked on both groups six months later to see how they were doing. The results were astonishing. Class participants reported healthier behaviors, better communication with their doctors, and most important, better health than the control group.[4]

Two years later, Lorig and her team followed up with the patients who had taken the classes. They found that they had largely maintained their behavior changes, which resulted in fewer outpatient and ER visits. As a result, the program saved the healthcare system $590 per person over two years—greater than the initial costs of the program.[5]

There are now multiple ways in which patients can get self-management training, including through group classes, individual classes, digital and in-person formats, and certified coaching. Yet despite the fact that this study was published almost two decades ago, self-management training—and health coaching more broadly—is not widely available and often poorly implemented.

REALIZING THE VISION

To realize the vision, patients will need many more tools and resources to manage their own health.

Information on Quality and Costs of Care

Key to my hypothetical prediabetes example was that you knew the prices of the different options for care before you made the decision, and based on this information, you decided that one of the options was out of your budget.

Today, patients often don't know the costs or the quality of healthcare services before they access them. Without this information, it's difficult to impossible to make informed decisions. The lack of transparency in healthcare is so great that it often deters patients from getting care—even when they can afford it—for fear of receiving a surprise bill afterward.

Quality data is sorely lacking. Where measures exist, they are difficult to understand because they are designed for doctors and administrators, not for patients. One area where investment is urgently needed is greater transparency in the experience of care. Healthcare should borrow measures like net promoter scores and customer satisfaction from industries with high levels of customer service.

Access to High-Quality Health Information

As was magnified at multiple points of the Covid-19 pandemic, misinformation from online sources and social media can have disastrous consequences.

One solution is to integrate high-quality sources of information like those provided by the CDC or Mayo Clinic into patient portals, apps, and services so that patients have ready access to vetted medical content. One intriguing innovation is to personalize people's searches based on their health information. For example, searching "What should I take for a headache?" would return different results for a person with no known medical conditions and a person with chronic kidney issues. In the latter case, the search results might exclude ibuprofen and other nonsteroidal inflammatory medications (NSAIDs), which can worsen kidney problems.

Another approach is to flag trusted (or mistrusted) sources of information. I still remember back in the early 2000s when I built my first website, Beyond Apples, a blog on preventive health. Wanting my blog to be seen as a trusted source of information, I applied for certification from Health On The Net, a nonprofit affiliated with the World Health Organization. A more recent version of this is what Twitter and other social media companies have done with verification badges. However, more rigorous—and ideally independent—standards are needed as patients increasingly access medical information online.

A Greater Role in Decision-Making

As I learned with my checklist, information won't be enough. To make informed choices, patients often need a little help to make the best decisions for their health. This will require new ways for doctors and healthcare professionals to educate, receive consent from, and partner with patients.

As part of my mom's diabetes reversal program, she was given patient videos to watch on her phone. Through the power of multimedia, in less than two hours, she went from barely having heard of a ketogenic diet to understanding the science behind it, the side effects to watch for, and the process for checking her own ketones. Had she received this education in clinic, it could have easily taken multiple visits over six to eight weeks and even then not have been as effective as video-based training.

It is also important for patients to understand the benefits and harms of medical care, even for relatively simple services like requesting an at-home test or a medication. A critical question in the shift to self-service is: How do we drive an efficient yet effective process to achieve informed consent? We've all had the experience of signing a terms of service agreement without having read any of it. While your cable service might not want you to read all the small print to become fully informed, your doctors have a vested interest in having you fully understand the potential benefits and risks of the treatment they are proposing, but often those details aren't easy to understand. One solution is to use graphical and video-based forms of informed consent, like those increasingly being used in research studies, which have been shown to lead to greater patient satisfaction and engagement.[6]

Taking these models to scale will require changing the culture of medicine. I still remember a patient of mine when I was at the University of Chicago, a professor, who refused to get a mammogram to screen for breast cancer. I was baffled at first, and as someone who had just written a book on preventive health, I was admittedly prideful and bullheaded in initially refusing to accept her decision. But over the course of multiple visits, she demonstrated how deeply she understood the risks and benefits of not getting screened for breast cancer. Mammograms aren't infallible. They certainly don't catch all breast cancers and often can't distinguish between high-risk and low-risk cancers, which sometimes leads to unnecessary biopsies and even unnecessary surgery and radiation. She was also worried about the pain and embarrassment of the test itself. She knew all the information and she knew herself, and she decided that mammography didn't make sense—at least for her. I couldn't argue with that.

Our job as healthcare professionals isn't to impose our preferences on others. Rather, it's to serve as a guide and help patients illuminate the benefits and harms of decisions for themselves and then, once made, to respect those decisions. This is a foundational idea in shared decision-making: patients and doctors make healthcare decisions together by taking into account the best scientific evidence as well as patients' values and preferences.

More Support for Managing Their Health

One of the dangers of a more patient-directed world is that it increases the burden on patients and their families, as I learned in my checklist study. This is particularly a concern for low-income patients, the elderly, and individuals with multiple chronic conditions, who have the greatest healthcare needs, yet most often lack the resources to manage them.

Patients will need a whole new set of services to navigate the system and support decision-making. For many patients, this coordination and advocacy function is well served by their physician. However, for many—arguably, most—patients, this will not be enough.

One model for supporting patients is to pair them with health advocates or patient navigators. At MetroHealth System in Cleveland, patients are provided a patient navigator to help them through their cancer journey from diagnosis to treatment. The navigators address barriers to care, including financial, logistical, emotional, and cultural. They build a trusting relationship with patients based on an understanding of their whole-person needs and then assist them with the logistics of care, from managing appointments and completing medical forms to making arrangements for transportation and securing childcare services to help them make it to their treatments. Their model has been shown to reduce no-show rates by 3 percent, reducing delays in care and also saving the health system money.[7]

The model also has the potential to reduce health disparities. Harold Freeman is an African American physician who first pioneered patient navigation two decades ago in Harlem Hospital Center. After he enrolled female patients—97 percent of whom were African American—in early breast-cancer detection programs and paired them with patient navigators, five-year sur-vival rates rose from 39 percent to 70 percent.[8]

Another example of this model is the health advocacy and care navigation services we discussed in Chapter 4 that are offered by forward-leaning employers.

Greater Autonomy to Direct Their Own Care

In certain cases, patients should be able to access a test or a med-ication without seeing a doctor first. To realize the potential of facilitated self-service, we need to rethink how we decide what treatments and tests to make directly available to patients. Too often our frame of reference is to compare the benefits and harms of patients being able to access a test or treatment without first seeing a doctor with the benefits and harms of accessing these through a doctor. But the unfortunate reality for many patients today is a third alternative—no care at all. To increase access to care, we need new regulatory frameworks that balance accessibil-ity with safety and efficacy.

Access to Doctors Who Match Their Preferences

Core to effective care is trusting, empathetic relationships between patients and their providers. As someone whose family immigrated from India, I see how my mom and many of my family members in her generation prefer seeing doctors of Indian descent. Having a doctor that she shares a common set of experi-ences with puts my mom at ease and makes her more comfortable opening up. It also makes her care more culturally tailored. My mom has diabetes and is a strict vegetarian who generally prefers Indian food. That her doctor follows a similar diet allows him to counsel her on which foods to eat and which to avoid.

Preferences vary widely—race ethnicity, language, culture, sexual orientation. Often, it just comes down to personality. As Harvard physician and researcher Ateev Mehrotra said, "We often have long discussions about not having enough primary care doctors in some communities. But one of the things that is often not said is that patients in a community, even though they have an ample supply of primary care providers, just don't like their primary care doctor."

Today, finding a doctor is a complex maze of checking insurance coverage and appointment availability. It's also relatively data-free. Often all patients know about me as a doctor is whether I'm in their insurance network and maybe what medical school I went to or my ratings on Google. But this is not the information they need. What they want to know is do I see patients like them and am I a doctor they can build a trusting relationship with?

This idea of patients seeing doctors who match their preferences and needs is grounded in research. Lisa Cooper is a primary care physician and researcher at Johns Hopkins who received a MacArthur "Genius" grant for demonstrating the role of patient-provider "concordance" on patient experience and outcomes. In a series of studies, she found that patients who had doctors who were concordant—matched in their race—experienced higher-quality communication with their doctors and rated the quality of their care more highly than did patients with discordant doctors.[9]

When I talked to Lisa about her research, she told me that it grew from a simple observation: "I noticed that the more you have in common with somebody, the more likely it is that you'll get to some of the major issues that might be impacting the patient's health." To realize this potential, we need to make it easier for patients to find doctors like them, and we need to expand the diversity of the health workforce to reflect the diversity of the community it serves.

The benefits of such an approach may extend beyond the individual patient-doctor interaction. "It could actually change the way the whole organization works," Lisa explained. "When you have more diverse people in the profession, that not only gives patients more choice but it could allow people who are underrepresented in the profession to be more a part of the way the organization works, whether they are working as frontline providers or driving the mission of the organization as leaders."

New Ways for Paying for Care

Patients today are limited to healthcare services that are covered by their employers or insurance companies, or that are offered free by their healthcare provider. This puts a wide range of services that could help them better manage their health out of reach, especially for our most vulnerable patients. For example, individuals with asthma can get expensive medications and several nights in the hospital paid for but not a carpet-cleaning service that could help avoid these costly interventions by reducing the dust and mites that trigger asthma episodes. One approach that is gaining traction in the United States is health savings accounts in which patients and employers can contribute dollars in a tax-advantaged way and then use those funds to cover a wide range of healthcare and nonhealthcare services, such as carpet cleaning. While useful, these approaches do little to help those who live paycheck to paycheck and lack the ability to save.

Another intriguing idea is to give patients money to decide for themselves where to get care. This approach has been piloted with breast pumps. Employers are now largely required to cover breast pumps for new mothers, but they frequently limit their choice to one pump, which often doesn't meet women's needs or preferences. Instead, what some innovative employers are doing is giving moms the equivalent of a gift card to buy any breast pump of their choice. If the pump they choose is more expensive, they pay the difference. This enables new moms to have far greater choice while still managing costs for the employer. The same idea could be explored for a broad range of healthcare services. In the case of my mother's diabetes reversal, she had to pay for the program out of her own pocket. Fortunately, we could afford it, but many patients can't. One could easily imagine an alternative model where she is given money equal to the cost of seeing a diabetes specialist, which her insurance company would cover, to pay for the reversal program.

A Voice in Healthcare Improvement

For far too long, healthcare has provided an abysmal patient experience. And for far too long, patients have been powerless to do anything about it. If care is truly to be patient-directed, patients should be given a voice in improving it.

This has been the case perhaps no more evidently than in low- and middle-income countries. In the public health systems that I've worked in when I was at the World Bank, healthcare workers often don't show up to work, and when they show up, they don't treat the patients very well. U-Report is a platform developed by UNICEF to enable people to speak out on issues that matter to them and to work for positive change in their community. Using a social messaging tool U-Report allows patients and families who have a poor experience with care to immediately report it. Whereas in the past, they would file a report on a piece of paper that would linger in the clinic for months or more often not make a report in the first place for fear of retribution, now patients can simply open an app or send a text message and share their concern in minutes with the appropriate people in the ministry of health to act on—similar to what happens with modern ticketing systems when you're locked out of your computer and your IT department resets your password.[10]

The end-user design perspective is needed to make these systems work. Nearly all of us have had the experience of being asked to fill out a survey and not doing it. MomConnect, an initiative of the South African National Department of Health, has found that you can't just ask patients to give you data. You need to first build a system that creates value for patients.

MomConnect is a digital platform developed with the primary intention of improving infant and maternal health. It provides pregnant women with a steady stream of information tailored to their stage of pregnancy—for example, the prenatal vitamins to take and healthy food choices. They can also ask questions about their health through a phone app.

Debbie Rogers, managing director of Praekelt.org, one of the key technical partners for MomConnect, told me that the app has almost a million active users and has become such a part of their everyday life that many wish MomConnect "good morning" and "good night." This kind of engagement allows MomConnect to fulfill its secondary intention, which is making South Africa's healthcare system better for patients. When MomConnect asks its users to complete a survey, they do it. And the data has been powerful. Debbie gave me an example of a time when the MomConnect community reported difficulty getting folic acid vitamins at their prenatal visits, well before any of the country's own surveillance systems detected a stockout. It's all part of a service that helps users stay socially connected and healthy. And there's no question that they love it. "Every Mothers' Day we're flooded with thank-you messages," Debbie told me.

Access to Their Own Data

Core to giving patients more control of their health is giving them access and ultimately ownership of their own data. The fact that in 2021 patients have to request their own health information is unacceptable.

Not only do patients have a right to their own data but having it also can impact their healthcare. I recently learned of a friend who had accessed the results of her blood test online. Fortunately, they indicated that she didn't have anemia, her primary concern, but she noticed that her doctor missed another finding in her lab work, which she then brought to his attention. Unfortunately, this isn't all that uncommon—7 percent of abnormal test results are lost to follow-up.[11]

While essential, access to health information is not sufficient. Patients shouldn't be left on their own to google the meaning of their own health information to make heads or tails of it. We need to present that information in a way that patients can understand.

STRATEGIC ACTIONS

The shift to patient-directed care will put patients in greater control of their health, which promises to dramatically improve the accessibility and experience of care. For patient-directed care to achieve its full potential, we need to thread the needle between the antiquated paternalism that is deeply ingrained in healthcare and the unfettered consumerism that works only for the few. Doing so will require new care models, tools, and payment models that put more resources, decision-making authority, and skills in the hands of patients and a system of care that is fundamentally simpler to navigate and use.

Here are some steps that all of us can take to accelerate our path to patient-directed care and position ourselves and our organizations to succeed.

Patients, Caregivers, and Consumers of Care

- Get a primary care doctor. See them when you're healthy so you can get up to date on your preventive care (vaccinations, cancer screenings, etc.) and establish goals for your physical and mental health.

- Invest in your health. Create an annual budget for your healthcare needs, including medical goods (a scale, thermometer, blood pressure machine), subscription services (gym membership, mental health coaching, telemedicine services), and copays and deductibles. Create time in your calendar to learn how to self-manage your conditions, understand your health data, and organize your healthcare.

- Collect and store your own healthcare data. This can be as simple as requesting your medical records after every visit and keeping a file at home. Increasingly, your records can also be downloaded from patient portals.

- Use consumer-friendly applications that can guide better decision-making, and take every opportunity to provide customer feedback on websites that evaluate hospitals, doctors, health plans, and other healthcare services.

- Demand to know how much you will have to spend out of pocket before agreeing to any test or medication.

- If you are more comfortable talking to a doctor who shares your racial, cultural, or gender identity or speaks your language, it's OK to find one that does. Trusting, empathetic relationships are central to healthcare, and your relationship with your doctor is paramount.

Physicians and Healthcare Professionals

- Curate patient materials, including video links, websites, and educational handouts, to give to patients who present with common conditions. For example, I keep handy printouts of exercises for knee pain in Spanish.

- Encourage patients to use your electronic health record's portal so they have direct access to their health information.

Healthcare Delivery Systems, Including Traditional and Technology Enabled

- Make it easy for patients to request their data. Better yet, automatically give it to them as part of every patient encounter.

- Implement a modern ticketing system for patients to provide feedback and then make reviewing critical tickets part of management meetings.

- Integrate shared decision-making into routine clinical practice by leveraging multimedia and integrating decision support into the electronic health record and clinical workflows. Survey patients on whether they were provided more than one option for their care and give that feedback to your doctors regularly.

- Offer your patients self-management training programs and set organizational goals for completion rates.

- Make it simpler for patients to understand your prices. Recognize that patients often won't get care for fear of a surprise bill. By standardizing and simplifying your prices, you can do the right thing—and improve your business.

- Build teams of patients, user experience designers, and clinicians to make healthcare simpler and more intuitive for patients to direct themselves.

- Develop a healthcare workforce that is reflective of the diversity of the population you serve.

Payers, Including Employers, Government Entities, and Health Plans

- Expand coverage for self-service tools that provide patients a safe and effective way to access common tests and medications.

- Invest in care navigation and advocacy services, especially if you have an older population or a population with multiple chronic care and social needs.

- Incorporate data on physicians' race, ethnicity, gender identity, and language into provider directories and search tools.

- Create new reimbursement models that put more dollars in the hands of patients to make their own care decisions.

- Demand that traditional and technology-enabled delivery systems implement patient experience measures and systems for receiving and responding to patient feedback.

Policymakers

- Remove obstacles to self-service models by creating frameworks for deciding which tests and medications require a physician to administer and what level of physician oversight is needed.

- Create a national model for vetting and trusting online medical information, including through the use of innovative public-private partnerships.

- Expand efforts like the National Diabetes Prevention Program to increase patient access to accredited self-management and other community-based care models.

- Mandate that delivery systems standardize and simplify the units and prices of healthcare services in terms that patients can understand.

- Spur investment in a personal health record that includes social needs assessment, goals for health, options for support from social service agencies, and recommendations for clinical care.

- Invest in a diverse health workforce—for example, by developing or expanding loan forgiveness programs for physicians and healthcare professionals who practice in underserved communities or who come from underrepresented minority communities.

Healthcare Investors and Entrepreneurs

Invest in and build companies that help patients to:

- Access high-quality health information.

- Access and understand their personal health data.

- Make informed decisions about their care using data on price, quality, and outcomes.

- Self-manage their preventive, chronic, and mental healthcare.

- Self-serve their healthcare needs.

- Engage and empower family, friends, and informal and formal caregivers.

- Link to social and community-based resources.

- Manage their healthcare budget and needs.

CONCLUSION

onths into the Covid-19 pandemic, I arrived at my clinic on the outskirts of Washington, DC. The new normal was settling in. As I drove into the parking lot, I waved to my clinic staff huddled under a white tent, waiting for the next patient to drive up and get tested. When I entered the building, a nurse checked my temperature and asked if I was having any symptoms before handing me a surgical mask. I walked through our largely empty waiting room with chairs six feet apart to the workroom where I'd spend most of my day seeing patients from my clinic mobile phone.

But when I logged into my electronic health record, something seemed very wrong. My schedule, which for the past several weeks had been filled with back-to-back appointments, nearly 25 to 30 patients a day, was nearly empty. I refreshed my screen, but nothing changed. I only had five patients for the entire day.

On one level, this was a good thing. After several weeks of intense effort, the public health community in our region had successfully gotten the first wave of Covid-19 under control. There were fewer cases and more places to get tested.

But on many levels, it was deeply troubling. For one, local reports showed that Covid-19 was continuing to wreak havoc among the most vulnerable members of our community. Case rates were high among essential workers, African Americans, Latinos, and families living in poverty. These were the very patients to whom my clinic, a federally qualified health center, was designed to provide free and low-cost care. And yet, we still weren't reaching them.

Equally concerning was the fact that I had so few patients on my schedule for non-Covid-19 concerns. Patients were not returning for their routine preventive and chronic care. Rates of vaccinations, cancer screenings, and follow-up visits for diabetes and chronic conditions had plummeted. Even though we had taken serious measures to make the clinic safe from Covid-19 and expanded virtual care options for all types of visits, patients were still not coming back.

There were patients in need. Yet here I was—a fully trained physician at a well-resourced clinic—waiting for patients to show up.

I started cold-calling patients to check in on them. I started with those I was most concerned about, patients with multiple chronic conditions or who had been recently discharged from the hospital. They were relieved to hear from me and thankful I had reached out.

In that moment of profound clarity, I realized something that not only was true in the midst of a global pandemic but—in many respects—had always been true: I wasn't the one waiting for my patients. My patients were waiting for me.

Outside my clinic walls a debate is raging about healthcare. On one side are people clamoring for expanded access to affordable care. We need more doctors. We need to lower healthcare costs. We need to end health disparities. On the other side are people clamoring for greater innovation. We need on-demand access to a doctor 24/7. We need more data. We need artificial intelligence.

Often, these debates occur at the extremes and in the abstract. Caught in the middle, as they often are, are patients and doctors, and the everyday issues that make the delivery of care fall far short of what's possible and what's needed.

What this book has presented is a framework for making healthcare work: Making it easier for patients to see a doctor who knows them. Helping patients adopt healthier behaviors and make better healthcare decisions. Giving doctors more time with their patients. Providing clinics resources to improve their practice. And most important, making healthcare human again.

As I've argued here, the future of healthcare must be distributed, digitally enabled, and decentralized. It's a future where care happens where health happens, at home and in the community; where patients and care teams are connected by data and technology that strengthen the relationships between them; and where decisions about care are made by those closest to it—doctors and patients. And it's a future that Covid-19 has made urgent, and in many respects, has also made possible.

This framework defines new concepts, not narrow solutions. Telemedicine is critical, but only if it distributes care to people who need it and is designed in a way that's comprehensive and integrated with their overall care needs. Digital solutions and data offer great promise, but they must enable trusting, empathetic relationships between patients and doctors and not replace them. Payment reform is desperately needed. However, it should not only shift responsibility and risk from insurers to health systems, but also decentralize resources and authority to the front lines of care. Implicit in this framework is the notion that it's not any one solution itself, but rather how these concepts are applied, that matters most. By focusing on clearly defined problems and designing solutions with input from patients, caregivers, and healthcare professionals, we can move the system forward.

Over my career, I've come to believe that real change in healthcare comes from changing the interactions between patients and their doctors, patients and their care teams, and patients and themselves. Changing those interactions requires new models of care that reimagine those interactions and do so in a way that improves health. To enable those models, we need new systems of care: new technologies, payment models, and training. To enable new systems of care, we need to improve the macroenvironment—new policies, regulation, and culture change.

But the history of healthcare is filled with examples of changes at the macro level that don't translate to changes at the micro level. The real work happens at the micro level, and it's at the micro level that our framework most applies.

As you leave this book and return to the work ahead, here's how this framework applies to the questions that are top of mind for you, for patients, and for healthcare leaders around the world.

MAKING HEALTHCARE MORE RESILIENT

The pandemic has rightfully led many policymakers and individuals to ask what we can do to better prepare for the next pandemic. Although it's been a century since the last truly global pandemic—the devastating Spanish influenza that lasted from 1918 to 1920—in the past 20 years we've had major outbreaks of Ebola, SARS, and H1N1, a trend we may only see more frequently as the world becomes ever more connected. Beyond epidemics, we can also expect more health emergencies from floods, wildfires, and environmental disasters, as the impact of climate change accelerates.[1]

Much of what's needed to prepare for these threats, including strengthening our public health infrastructure, disease surveillance, and supply chains, is beyond the scope of this book. But one thing we need for certain is a healthcare delivery system that is more resilient.

When care is concentrated in hospitals and clinics and suddenly these facilities are at capacity or are no longer places patients can safely enter, the entire system falls apart. This is the equivalent of putting all of our eggs in one basket; if the basket falls, all of our eggs break. That's why distributing resources as widely as possible is a basic tenet of disaster preparation. When care is distributed throughout communities and into homes, the system naturally becomes more resilient.

During Covid-19, we also saw how harmful misinformation was to our response.[2] Part of the problem was that we lacked a trusted voice to deliver health information. Doctors and nurses are consistently ranked the most trusted people in society,[3] but they are typically limited to engaging one patient at a time in a clinic setting. By digitally enabling care and making care more continuous, we can give the medical community a direct channel for relaying timely and accurate information to a broader population.

Decentralization is also essential. Empowering frontline health workers with authority and resources enables the system to be more agile. We saw this in the example of community health workers in post-cyclone Mozambique who were able to respond to stockouts and unforeseen challenges on the ground, and during the pandemic with clinics who, once freed from regulatory barriers, rapidly moved to providing virtual care to tens of millions of Americans.

EXPANDING ACCESS TO CARE FOR ALL

Healthcare is a human right. The fact that millions of Americans and people around the world lack access to affordable, high-quality care is unacceptable.

The current debate in the United States is largely focused on health insurance coverage. Much of this debate is outside the scope of this book. However, there are at least two problems that this book directly addresses. The first is that healthcare is unaffordable. In my experience, most employers want to provide health insurance for their employees, and most patients who are uninsured want to have health insurance. The problem is that they can't afford it. And the reason they can't afford it is because healthcare itself is too expensive. There is the oft-cited statistic that of the $4 trillion the United States spends on healthcare,

$1 trillion is waste[4]—the "tape worm" of the US economy as Warren Buffett once quipped.[5] The second is that insurance coverage is not enough. As many people with health insurance who have tried to find a doctor know, coverage does not equal access. It also certainly does not equal high-quality care.

As a common saying in healthcare goes, "Every system is perfectly designed to achieve the results it gets." The high costs, inaccessibility, and poor quality of care we have is the result of our system. Fix the system and you fix the problem. The question is, "How you do fix the system?"

The answer is to make the system more distributed, digitally enabled, and decentralized. Distributing care to the community and home is much less costly than providing these services in a clinic or hospital. As we discussed in Chapter 3, Bruce Leff's research at Johns Hopkins has shown that hospitalizing patients at home is 30 to 40 percent less expensive than hospital-based admissions, and with fewer complications and better outcomes for patients.[6] Using technology to make care more continuous drives behavior change, which reduces downstream costs and complications. The text-message-based diabetes program described in Chapter 5 lowered healthcare costs by over 8 percent while increasing glucose control and patient satisfaction.[7] Decentralizing resources to frontline health workers drives better health outcomes and lower costs, as we saw in Chapter 9 with Oak Street Health, a risk-based primary care clinic. Empowering patients with more skills and tools can prevent and reverse chronic health problems like my mom's type 2 diabetes.

By reinventing how care is delivered, we can unlock better health outcomes for all while enabling the expansion of affordable health coverage for those who are too often left out.

REDUCING HEALTH DISPARITIES

Many of the deep inequities faced by black and brown communities, immigrants, LGBTQ communities, individuals with disabilities, individuals living in poverty, rural communities, and other vulnerable health populations are due to structural failures outside of healthcare system, including unstable housing, lack of employment, fewer opportunities for education, and systemic racism. These can and must be addressed. In addition, the healthcare system itself is a major contributor to health disparities.

What I've seen time and time again in my career caring for underserved communities in East Baltimore, the South Side of Chicago, and Washington, DC, is that how seemingly intractable problems that affect my most vulnerable patients can be addressed by reinventing how care is delivered. As I mentioned in Chapter 2, during Covid-19 I saw my clinic's no-show rates plummet from as high as 20 percent to nearly zero as care went virtual. Although the reasons my patients struggled to access care—lack of paid time off, unstable transportation, childcare responsibilities, mistrust of the system—were unchanged, simply making care virtual and bringing care to patients rather than requiring patients to come to care helped overcome many of these barriers. Similarly, while the challenges of managing diabetes as an African American on the South Side of Chicago—lack of access to care, food deserts, poor walkability, low health literacy, high stress—are overwhelming, we saw that our text-message-based diabetes program, in which two-thirds of participants were African American, was able to dramatically improve health outcomes.

While the potential for the shifts outlined here to reduce disparities exists, it won't happen automatically. I've made the case throughout this book it must be deliberately designed and planned for. As my colleague at the World Bank, Jumana Qamruddin—an expert in scaling user-centered design—told me, "Designing solutions for the easier to reach patients and then adapting the system afterward for everyone else can result in leaving the most vulnerable behind. It's much harder to retrofit existing systems and solutions to be equitable and inclusive. If you want a system to be equitable and inclusive, it has to be core to your design from the start."

IMPROVING GLOBAL HEALTH

This framework can also assist low- and middle-income countries combat the big three infectious diseases (HIV/AIDS, malaria, and tuberculosis), unacceptable levels of maternal and child mortality, and rising levels of noncommunicable diseases (heart disease, diabetes, lung disease, and cancer).[8]

To many of my former colleagues at the World Bank and across the world, the idea of distributed care won't be new. Legendary physician and global health activist Paul Farmer describes the model of care of Partners in Health, the nonprofit he founded, as "community-based, health center-enriched, hospital-linked."[9] Over the years, Partners in Health has dramatically improved outcomes for HIV/AIDS and tuberculosis in some of the poorest places in the world. But his vision remains elusive. What I found at the World Bank was that ministries of finance are too often more apt to fund hospitals and facilities than community health worker programs like the one I encountered in Mozambique.

There is also a tremendous opportunity for global health to become digitally enabled. Africa is now the youngest continent on earth, with 60 percent of the population under age 25.[10] Increasingly, mobile phones, text messaging, and WhatsApp have become necessities for individuals living in poverty—these digital tools are now how they bank, how they find work, and how they stay connected to loved ones. There are a myriad of examples of efforts to build on these technologies—from hundreds of thousands of ASHA workers in India who use mobile phones to direct the care of mothers and children,[11] to the partnership between the Rwandan government and Babylon Health, a UK-based healthcare AI company, to provide telemedicine services,[12] to the MomConnect program for pregnant mothers in South Africa that we covered in Chapter 10.[13]

To achieve a vision of universal health, we also need to decentralize power to the community level. In global health, there is a long history of highly verticalized disease programs that elicit responses from donors rather than address the needs of communities. To reverse this, we must leapfrog over the facility- and physician-centered care models we've built in the United States and elsewhere and develop a comprehensive model of primary care and community health that empowers frontline health workers and patients.

REBUILDING RELATIONSHIPS
IN MEDICINE

In many respects, over the past decade, technology has gotten in the way of doctors and patients. In our exam rooms, we now have an intrusive piece of software—the electronic health record—that preoccupies and frustrates physicians and prevents us from building the trusting, caring relationships that are central to healthcare. At the same time, the proliferation of standalone telemedicine companies, pharmacies, and big box retailers that are getting into healthcare delivery has resulted in greater fragmentation than ever. And at least before the pandemic, AI loomed large in the minds of physicians as an existential threat to their profession.

The vision that I present here is directed toward addressing many of these concerns. If designed correctly, virtual, community, and home-based care should extend the reach of doctors into the home, ensuring that more care is provided by the same doctor, strengthening longitudinal relationships. Better software would free doctors from administrative tasks and enable them to more fully engage with their patients inside and outside of the clinic. Decision-making and resources will increasingly be in the hands of doctors, enabling them to regain control of the healthcare system and decide how best to serve their communities.

Realizing this vision will require nothing short of a transformation in the healthcare system. But as the world witnessed during Covid-19, healthcare workers are up to the challenge.

ASSURING THE HEALTH AND WELL-BEING OF OURSELVES AND OUR LOVED ONES

Perhaps more than anything else, Covid-19 has been a reminder that we are ultimately responsible for our own health—that it is in our hands, sometimes literally.

Our daily behaviors—how we live, what we eat, how we manage stress—have a major impact on our health and well-being and are the factors most within our control. As the system becomes more distributed, digitally enabled, and decentralized, patients will have access to more resources and tools to manage their health and healthcare. In this new world, patients will have a significant role to play in setting aside a budget for their health, maintaining their health information, and identifying the right doctors, care teams, and tools to support them. While these changes are largely positive, for some patients, there is a real risk of becoming overburdened or being excluded—issues that the health system will need to proactively address as I've outlined throughout the book.

Today, patients have the ability to see a primary care doctor online, request and store their health information, and verify that the care they are receiving is evidence-based—but too few are benefiting from it. As the system is transformed, it will be essential for patients to embrace change. A good place to start is by asking ourselves whether our current healthcare provider is meeting our needs; whether we are fully leveraging the resources available to us through our clinics, our employers, and our communities; and whether we are investing enough of our own time and resources toward our health.

CARE AFTER COVID

We are at an inflection point—one created by a global pandemic but now completely in our hands.

My greatest hope in writing this book is that it offers health-care leaders and patients a clear-eyed view of where healthcare needs to go and a scaffolding on which to build and implement their own ideas.

I'm well aware this work is not easy. There is tremendous uncertainty and risk we all face as we chart a new path forward. In my most trying moments, what I find clarifying now—and I hope for the rest of my career—is remembering this pandemic.

I'll remember the countless lives we lost and that were upended by this terrible calamity.

I'll remember the sacrifices of Dr. Li Wenliang, the Chinese physician who first sounded the alarm that a new pandemic was coming, and of healthcare workers around the world who died on the front lines.

I'll remember the relentless ingenuity of doctors, nurses, pharmacists, healthcare workers, healthcare administrators, and policymakers who came together in that moment to turn an entire system of care on its head.

It's for all of these people that this book is written and from whom the work in front of us to reinvent the healthcare system takes on its greatest meaning.

As Covid-19 has shown us all too vividly, this work matters. Our work matters. The health and well-being of millions of people depend on it.

Our patients are waiting. There isn't a moment to lose.

NOTES

INTRODUCTION
1. Sheri Fink, "Worst-Case Estimates for U.S. Coronavirus Deaths," *New York Times*, March 13, 2020, https://www.nytimes.com/2020/03/13/us /coronavirus-deaths-estimate.html.
2. World Health Organization, "Q&A on Coronaviruses (Covid-19)," April 17, 2020, https://www.who.int/emergencies/diseases/novel-coronavirus -2019/question-and-answers-hub/q-a-detail/q-a-coronaviruses.
3. Shantanu Nundy and Kavita Patel, "Self-Service Diagnosis of Covid-19: Ready for Prime Time?" *JAMA Health Forum*, March 16, 2020, https:// jamanetwork.com/channels/health-forum/fullarticle/2763264.
4. America Counts Staff, "One in Five Americans Live in Rural Areas," US Census Bureau, August 9, 2017, https://www.census.gov/library/stories /2017/08/rural-america.html.
5. US Census Bureau, "American Community Survey: Selected Housing Characteristics, 2018," accessed November 4, 2020, https://data.census.gov /cedsci/table?d=ACS%205-Year%20Estimates%20Data%20Profiles&tid= ACSDP5Y2018.DP04.
6. Shantanu Nundy, "Let Home Be Where the Hospital Is," *Washington Post*, April 16, 2020, https://www.washingtonpost.com/opinions/2020/03 /20/coronavirus-is-upending-society-here-are-ideas-mitigate-its-impact/ ?arc404=true.
7. Shantanu Nundy and Neeti Sanyal, "How to Make At-Home Coronavirus Testing Work," *Harvard Business Review*, March 24, 2020, https://hbr.org /2020/03/how-to-make-at-home-coronavirus-testing-work.
8. Stephen M. Hahn and Judith A. McMeekin, "Coronavirus (Covid-19) Update: FDA Alerts Consumers About Unauthorized Fraudulent Covid-19 Test Kits," *US Food and Drug Administration*, March 20, 2020, https:// www.fda.gov/news-events/press-announcements/coronavirus-covid-19 -update-fda-alerts-consumers-about-unauthorized-fraudulent-covid-19-test -kits.
9. US Food and Drug Administration, "Coronavirus (Covid-19) Update: FDA Authorizes First Test for Patient At-Home Sample Collection," *US Food and Drug Administration*, April 21, 2020, https://www.fda.gov/news -events/press-announcements/coronavirus-covid-19-update-fda-authorizes -first-test-patient-home-sample-collection.
10. US Department of Health & Human Services, "Notification of Enforcement Discretion for Telehealth Remote Communications During the Covid-19 Public Emergency," March 30, 2020, https://www.hhs.gov/hipaa/for-professionals/special-topics/emergency -preparedness/notification-enforcement-discretion-telehealth/index.html.

CHAPTER 1

1. Michelle L. Holshue, Chas DeBolt, M.P.H., Scott Lindquist, Kathy H. Lofy, John Wiesman, Hollianne Bruce, Christopher Spitters, Keith Ericson, Sara Wilkerson, Ahmet Tural, George Diaz, Amanda Cohn, et al. for the Washington State 2019-nCoV Case Investigation Team, "First Case of 2019 Novel Coronavirus in the United States," *New England Journal of Medicine*, March 5, 2020, https://doi.org/10.1056/NEJMoa2001191.

2. Nathan W. Furukawa, John T. Brooks, and Jeremy Sobel, "Evidence Supporting Transmission of Severe Acute Respiratory Syndrome Coronavirus 2 While Presymptomatic or Asymptomatic," *Centers for Disease Control and Prevention*, July 2020, https://wwwnc.cdc.gov/eid/article/26/7/20-1595_article.

3. "Similarities and Differences Between Flu and Covid-19," *Centers for Disease Control and Prevention*, accessed November 4, 2020, https://www.cdc.gov/flu/symptoms/flu-vs-Covid19.htm.

4. CDC Covid-19 Response Team, "Severe Outcomes Among Patients with Coronavirus Disease 2019 (Covid-19)—United States, February 12–March 16, 2020," *Morbidity and Mortality Weekly Report* 69, March 27, 2020, 343–346, http://dx.doi.org/10.15585/mmwr.mm6912e2.

5. Roni Caryn Rabin, "Nearly All Patients Hospitalized with Covid-19 Had Chronic Health Issues, Study Finds," *New York Times*, April 23, 2020, https://www.nytimes.com/2020/04/23/health/coronavirus-patients-risk.html.

6. "Covid-19 in Racial and Ethnic Minority Groups," *Centers for Disease Control and Prevention*, June 25, 2020, https://www.cdc.gov/coronavirus/2019-ncov/need-extra-precautions/racial-ethnic-minorities.html.

7. Hilary Bower, Sembia Johnson, Mohamed S. Bangura, Alie Joshua Kamara, Osman Kamara, Saidu H. Mansaray, Daniel Sesay, Cecilia Turay, Francesco Checchi, and Judith R. Glynn, "Exposure-Specific and Age-Specific Attack Rates for Ebola Virus Disease in Ebola-Affected Households, Sierra Leone," *NCBI*, August 22, 2016, https://www.ncbi.nlm.nih.gov/pmc/articles/PMC4982163/.

8. Alyssa Parpia, Martial Ndeffo-Mbah, Natasha Wenzel, and Alison Galvan, "Effects of Response to 2014–2015 Ebola Outbreak on Deaths from Malaria, HIV/AIDS, and Tuberculosis, West Africa." *Emerging Infectious Diseases* 22, March 2016, 433–441, https://doi.org/10.3201/eid2203.150977.

9. Shantanu Nundy, Manmeet Kaur, and Prabhjot Singh, "Preparing for and Responding to Covid-19's 'Second Hit,'" *Healthcare* 8, December 2020, https://doi.org/10.1016/j.hjdsi.2020.100461.

10. Association of American Medical Colleges, *The Complexities of Physician Supply and Demand: Projections from 2018 to 2023*, Washington, DC, accessed November 4, 2020, https://www.aamc.org/system/files/2020-06/stratcomm-aamc-physician-workforce-projections-june-2020.pdf.

11. Lisa Rosenbaum, "The Untold Toll—the Pandemic's Effects on Patients without Covid-19," *New England Journal of Medicine* 38, June 11, 2020, https:doi.org/10.1056/NEJMms2009984.

12. Epic Health Research Network, "Delayed Cancer Screenings," May 4, 2020, https://www.ehrn.org/articles/delays-in-preventive-cancer-screenings-during-covid-19-pandemic.

13. Jeanne Santoli, Megan Lindley, Malini DeSilva, Elyse Kharbanda, Matthew Daley, Lisa Galloway, Julianne Gee, Mick Glover, Ben Herring, Yoonjae Kang, Paul Lucas, Cameron Noblit, Jeanne Tropper, Tara Vogt,

and Eric Weintraub, "Effects of the Covid-19 Pandemic on Routine Pediatric Vaccine Ordering and Administration—United States," *Morbidity and Mortality Weekly Report* 69, May 15, 2020, 591–593, https://dx.doi.org/10.15585/mmwr.mm6919e2.

14. Ateev Mehrotra, Michael Chernew, David Linetsky, Hilary Hatch, and David Cutler, "The Impact of the Covid-19 Pandemic on Outpatient Visits: A Rebound Emerges," *The Commonwealth Fund*, May 19, 2020, https://www.commonwealthfund.org/publications/2020/apr/impact-covid-19-outpatient-visits.

15. Jacob Stern, "This Is Not a Normal Mental-Health Disaster," *Atlantic*, July 7, 2020, https://www.theatlantic.com/health/archive/2020/07/coronavirus-special-mental-health-disaster/613510/.

16. Martin Luther King, Jr, presentation at the Second National Convention of the Medical Committee for Human Rights, Chicago, Associated Press, March 26, 1966, https://pnhp.org/news/dr-martin-luther-king-on-health-care-injustice/.

17. Stephen Mein, "Covid-19 and Health Disparities: The Reality of 'the Great Equalizer,'" *Journal of General Internal Medicine* 35, August 2020, 2439–2440, https://dx.doi.org/10.1007/s11606-020-05880-5.

18. William Owen, Richard Carmona, and Claire Pomeroy, "Failing Another National Stress Test on Health Disparities," *Journal of the American Medical Association* 323, April 15, 2020, 1905–1906, https://doi.org/10.1001/jama.2020.6547.

19. Samantha Artiga and Kendal Orgera, "Covid-19 Presents Significant Risks for American Indian and Alaska Native People," *Kaiser Family Foundation*, May 14, 2020, https://www.kff.org/coronavirus-Covid-19/issue-brief/Covid-19-presents-significant-risks-for-american-indian-and-alaska-native-people/.

20. "Covid-19: Health Equity Concerns in Racial and Ethnic Minority Groups," *Centers for Disease Control and Prevention*, July 24, 2020, https://www.cdc.gov/coronavirus/2019-ncov/need-extra-precautions/racial-ethnic-minorities.html.

21. Michele K. Evans, Lisa Rosenbaum, Debra Malina, Stephen Morrissey, and Eric J. Rubin, "Diagnosing and Treating Systemic Racism," *New England Journal of Medicine* 383, July 16, 2020, 274–276, https://doi.org/10.1056/NEJMe2021693.

22. "Covid-19 and Minority Health Access," *Rubix Life Sciences,* March 2020, https://rubixls.com/wp-content/uploads/2020/04/COVID-19-Minority-Health-Access-7-1.pdf.

23. Sandra G. Boodman, "Spurred by Convenience, Millennials Often Spurn the 'Family Doctor' Model," *Kaiser Health News*, October 9, 2018, https://khn.org/news/spurred-by-convenience-millennials-often-spurn-the-family-doctor-model/.

24. "Too Many People Living with HIV in the U.S. Don't Know It," HIV.gov, June 10, 2019, https://www.hiv.gov/blog/too-many-people-living-hiv-us-don-t-know-it.

25. "National Diabetes Statistics Report 2020," *Centers for Disease Control*, accessed November 4, 2020, https://www.cdc.gov/diabetes/pdfs/data/statistics/national-diabetes-statistics-report.pdf.

26. "Online Summary of Trends in US Cancer Control Measures," *National Cancer Institute,* March 2020, https://progressreport.cancer.gov/diagnosis/stage.

27. PatientCareLink, "Healthcare-Acquired Infections (HAIs)," *2020 Massachusetts Health & Hospital Association, Inc.*, accessed November 4, 2020, https://patientcarelink.org/improving-patient-care/healthcare-acquired -infections-hais/#:~:text=In percent20American percent20hospitals percent t20alone percent2C percent20the,percent percent20are percent20surgical percent20site percent20infections.

28. Michael Daniel, "Study Suggests Medical Errors Now Third Leading Cause of Death in the U.S.," *John Hopkins Medicine*, May 3, 2016, https://www .hopkinsmedicine.org/news/media/releases/study_suggests_medical_errors _now_third_leading_cause_of_death_in_the_us.

29. "Estimates of Influenza Vaccination Coverage Among Adults—United States, 2017–18 Flu Season," *Centers for Disease Control*, October 25, 2018, https://www.cdc.gov/flu/fluvaxview/coverage-1718estimates.htm.

30. Ingrid J. Hall, Florence K.L. Tangka, Susan A. Sabatino, Trevor D. Thompson, Barry I. Graubard, and Nancy Breen, "Patterns and Trends in Cancer Screening in the United States," *Preventing Chronic Disease*, July 26, 2018, http://dx.doi.org/10.5888/pcd15.170465.

31. "Facts & Statistics: Physical Activity," HHS.gov, January 26, 2017, https:// www.hhs.gov/fitness/resource-center/facts-and-statistics/index.html.

32. US Department of Health and Human Services, "Current Eating Patterns in the United States," *2015–2020 Dietary Guidelines for Americans* 38, Fig. 2-1. https://health.gov/sites/default/files/2019-09/2015-2020_Dietary _Guidelines.pdf.

33. Centers for Disease Control and Prevention, "Smoking Is Down, but Almost 38 Million American Adults Still Smoke," January 18, 2018, https:// www.cdc.gov/media/releases/2018/p0118-smoking-rates-declining.html.

34. David R. Williams and Lisa A. Cooper, "Covid-19 and Health Equity—a New Kind of 'Herd Immunity,'" *Journal of the American Medical Association* 323, May 11, 2020, 2478–2480, https://doi.org/10.1001/jama.2020 .8051.

35. Linda Villarosa, "Why American's Black Mothers and Babies Are in a Life-or-Death Crisis," *New York Times Magazine*, April 11, 2020, https://www .nytimes.com/2018/04/11/magazine/black-mothers-babies-death-maternal -mortality.html.

36. Office of Minority Health, "Diabetes and African Americans," *US Department of Health and Human Services*, December 19, 2019, https:// minorityhealth.hhs.gov/omh/browse.aspx?lvl=4&lvlid=18.

37. CDC Newsroom, "Racial and Ethnic Disparities Continue in Pregnancy-Related Deaths," *Centers for Disease Control*, September 5, 2019, https:// www.cdc.gov/media/releases/2019/p0905-racial-ethnic-disparities -pregnancy-deaths.html.

38. Assistant Secretary for Public Affairs, "Telehealth: Delivering Care Safely During Covid-19," *US Department of Health and Human Services*, accessed November 4, 2020, https://www.hhs.gov/coronavirus/telehealth /index.html.

39. Sarah Maslin Nir, "In Virus Hot Spot, Lining Up and Anxious at Drive-in Test Center," *New York Times*, March 17, 2020, https://www.nytimes.com /2020/03/17/nyregion/new-rochelle-coronavirus-testing.html.

40. Bruce Japsen, "Amazon's Coronavirus Testing for Workers Remains Rare Move by an Employer," *Forbes*, June 10, 2020, https://www.forbes.com /sites/brucejapsen/2020/06/10/amazons-coronavirus-testing-for-workers -remains-rare-move-by-an-employer/#ae6e69b39b84.

PART 1

1. Bruce Leff, "Defining and Disseminating the Hospital-at-Home Model," *Canadian Medical Association Journal* 180, January 20, 2009, 156–157, https://doi.org/10.1503/cmaj.081891.
2. Christine Vestal, "To Speed up Results, States Limit Covid-19 Testing," *PEW*, August 14, 2020, https://www.pewtrusts.org/en/research-and-analysis /blogs/stateline/2020/08/14/to-speed-up-results-states-limit-covid-19-testing.

CHAPTER 2

1. Lev Facher, "9 Ways Covid-19 May Forever Upend the U.S. Health Care Industry," *STAT News*, May 19, 2020, https://www.statnews.com/2020/05 /19/9-ways-covid-19-forever-upend-health-care/.
2. Oleg Bestsennyy, Greg Gilbert, Alex Harris, and Jennifer Rost, "Telehealth: A Quarter-Trillion-Dollar Post-Covid-19 Reality?" *McKinsey & Company*, May 29, 2020, https://www.mckinsey.com/industries/healthcare -systems-and-services/our-insights/telehealth-a-quarter-trillion-dollar-post -covid-19-reality.
3. Stephanie Knaak, Ed Mantler, and Andrew Szeto, "Mental Illness-Related Stigma in Healthcare," *Healthcare Management Forum* 30, March 2017, 111–116, https://doi.org/10.1177/0840470416679413.
4. "Important Milestones: Your Child by Four Years," *Centers for Disease Control and Prevention*, June 9, 2020, https://www.cdc.gov/ncbddd/actearly /milestones/milestones-4yr.html.
5. Eric Roberts and Ateev Mehrotra, "Assessment of Disparities in Digital Access Among Medicare Beneficiaries and Implications for Telemedicine," *JAMA Internal Medicine* 180, October 2020, 1386–1389, https://doi.org /10.1001/jamainternmed.2020.2666.
6. David Velasquez and Ateev Mehrotra, "Ensuring the Growth of Telehealth During Covid-19 Does Not Exacerbate Disparities in Care," *Health Affairs Blog*, May 8, 2020, https://www.healthaffairs.org/do/10.1377 /hblog20200505.591306/full/.
7. Kurt C. Stange, "Barbara Starfield: Passage of the Pathfinder of Primary Care," *Annals of Family Medicine* 9, July 2011, 292–296, https://doi.org/ 10.1370/afm.1293.
8. Eric Wicklund, "Teledermatology Scores Big with Doctors and Patients," *mHealth Intelligence*, July 5, 2016, https://mhealthintelligence.com/news /teledermatology-scores-big-with-doctors-and-patients.
9. Zsolt Kulcsar, Daniel Albert, Ellyn Ercolano, and John N Mecchella, "Telerheumatology: A Technology Appropriate for Virtually All," *Seminars in Arthritis and Rheumatology* 46, December 2016, 380–385, https://doi.org /10.1016/j.semarthrit.2016.05.013.
10. Kat Jercich, "The Successes—and Pitfalls—of Using Telehealth for Home-Based Primary Care," *Healthcare IT News*, June 26, 2020, https://www .healthcareitnews.com/news/successes-and-pitfalls-using-telehealth-home -based-primary-care.

CHAPTER 3

1. Samantha Artiga and Elizabeth Hinton, "Beyond Healthcare: The Role of Social Determinants in Promoting Health and Health Equity," *Kaiser Family Foundation*, May 10, 2018, https://www.kff.org/racial-equity-and-health -policy/issue-brief/beyond-health-care-the-role-of-social-determinants-in -promoting-health-and-health-equity/.

2. "Ready Responders," accessed November 4, 2020: https://readyresponders.com/.

3. Brian Rosenthal, Joseph Goldstein, and Michael Rothfeld, "Coronavirus in N.Y.: 'Deluge' of Cases Begins Hitting Hospitals," *New York Times*, March 21, 2020, https://www.nytimes.com/2020/03/20/nyregion/ny-coronavirus-hospitals.html.

4. Shantanu Nundy and Kavita K. Patel, "Hospital-at-Home to Support Covid-19 Surge—Time to Bring Down the Walls?" *JAMA Health Forum*, May 1, 2020, https://doi.org/10.1001/jamahealthforum.2020.0504.

5. Robert Holly, "Mount Sinai at Home, Other Hospital-at-Home Models Proving Value Amid National Emergency," *Home Healthcare News*, April 7, 2020, https://homehealthcarenews.com/2020/04/mount-sinai-at-home-other-hospital-at-home-models-proving-value-amid-national-emergency/.

6. Institute of Medicine (US) Committee on Quality of Healthcare in America, Linda T. Kohn, Janet M. Corrigan, and Molla S. Donaldson, eds., *To Err Is Human: Building a Safer Health System*," November 1999, https://www.nap.edu/catalog/9728/to-err-is-human-building-a-safer-health-system.

7. Bruce Leff and Lynda Burton, "Future Directions: Alternative Approaches to Traditional Hospital Care—Home Hospital," *Clinics in Geriatric Medicine* 14, November 1998: 851–862, https://doi.org/10.1016/S0749-0690(18)30095-8.

8. Bruce Leff, Lynda Burton, Scott L. Mader, Jeffrey Burl, Rebecca Clark, William B. Greenough III, Susan Guido, Donald Steinwachs, John R. Burton, "Satisfaction with Hospital at Home Care," *Journal of the American Geriatric Society* 54, September 2006, 1355–1363, https://doi.org/10.1111/j.1532-5415.2006.00855.x.

9. Bruce Leff, Lynda Burton, and Scott L. Mader, "Hospital at Home: Feasibility and Outcomes of a Program to Provide Hospital-Level Care at Home for Acutely Ill Older Patients," *Annals of Internal Medicine* 143, December 6, 2005, 143, 798–808, https://doi.org/10.7326/0003-4819-143-11-200512060-00008.

10. Stacy Weiner, "Interest in Hospital-at-Home Programs Explodes During Covid-19," AAMC, September 29, 2020, https://www.aamc.org/news-insights/interest-hospital-home-programs-explodes-during-covid-19.

11. "Medically Home," accessed November 4, 2020, https://www.medicallyhome.com/about-us/.

PART 2

1. David E. Arterburn, Andy Bogart, Nancy E. Sherwood, Stephen Sidney, Karen J. Coleman, Sebastien Haneuse, Patrick J. O'Connor, Mary Kay Theis, Guilherme M. Campos, David McCulloch, and Joe Selby, "A Multisite Study of Long-Term Remission and Relapse of Type 2 Diabetes Mellitus Following Gastric Bypass," *Obesity Surgery* 23, January 2013, 93–102, https://doi.org/10.1007/s11695-012-0802-1.

2. John B. Buse, Sonia Caprio, William T. Cefalu, Antonio Ceriello, Stefano Del Prato, Silvio E. Inzucchi, Sue McLaughlin, Gordon L. Phillips II, R. Paul Robertson, Francesco Rubino, Richard Kahn, and M. Sue Kirkman, "How Do We Define Cure of Diabetes?" *Diabetes Care* 32, November 2009, 2133–2135, https://doi.org/10.2337/dc09-9036.

3. Andrew J. Karter, Shantanu Nundy, Melissa M. Parker, Howard H. Moffet, and Elbert S. Huang, "Incidence of Remission in Adults with Type 2 Diabetes: The Diabetes & Aging Study," *Diabetes Care* 37, December 2014, 3188–3195, https://dx.doi.org/10.2337/dc14-0874.

4. Shaminie J. Athinarayanan, Rebecca Adams, Sarah Hallberg, Amy McKenzie, Nasir Bhanpuri, Wayne Campbell, Jeff Volek, Stephen Phinney, and James McCarter, "Long Term Effects of a Novel Continuous Remote Care Intervention Including Nutritional Ketosis for the Management of Type 2 Diabetes: A 2-Year Non-randomized Clinical Trial," *Frontiers in Endocrinology*, June 5, 2019, https://doi.org/10.3389/fendo.2019.00348.
5. Virta, "How It Works," *Virta Health Corp*, 2020, accessed November 4, 2020, https://www.virtahealth.com/howitworks.

CHAPTER 4

1. David Levine, Jeffrey Linder, and Bruce Landon, "Characteristics of Americans with Primary Care and Changes Over Time, 2002–2015," *JAMA Internal Medicine* 180, January 20, 2020, 463–466, https://doi.org/10.1001/jamainternmed.2019.6282.
2. Patti Neighmond, "Can't Get in to See Your Doctor? Many Patients Turn to Urgent Care," *NPR*, March 7, 2016, https://www.npr.org/sections/health-shots/2016/03/07/469196691/cant-get-in-to-see-your-doctor-many-patients-turn-to-urgent-care.
3. Scott Vold, "3 Important Statistics About Provider Referrals," *Becker's Healthcare*, August 11, 2016, https://www.beckershospitalreview.com/payer-issues/3-important-statistics-about-provider-referrals.html.
4. "Chesapeake Regional Information System for Our Patients," *CRISP Health*, 2020, accessed November 3, 2020, https://crisphealth.org.

CHAPTER 5

1. Jonathan J. Dick, Shantanu Nundy, Marla C. Solomon, Keisha N. Bishop, Marshall H. Chin, and Monica E. Peek, "Feasibility and Usability of a Text-Based Program for Diabetes Self-Management in an Urban African-American Population," *Journal of Diabetes Science and Technology* 5, September 1, 2011, 1246–54, https://doi.org/10.1177/193229681100500534.
2. Shantanu Nundy, Jonathan J. Dick, Anna P. Goddu, Patrick Hogan, Chen-Yuan E. Lu, Marla C. Solomon, Arnell Bussie, Marshall H. Chin, and Monica E. Peek, "Using Mobile Health to Support the Chronic Care Model: Developing an Institutional Initiative," *International Journal of Telemedicine and Applications*, December 5, 2012, https://doi.org/10.1155/2012/871925.
3. Shantanu Nundy, Jonathan J. Dick, Chia-Hung Chou, Robert S. Nocon, Marshall H. Chin, and Monica E. Peek, "Mobile Phone Diabetes Project Led to Improved Glycemic Control and Net Savings for Chicago Plan Participants," *Health Affairs* 33, February 2014, 265–72, https://doi.org/10.1377/hlthaff.2013.0589.
4. Ross Hilliard, Jacqueline Haskell, and Rebekah Gardner, "Are Specific Elements of Electronic Health Record Use Associated with Clinician Burnout More Than Others?" *Journal of the American Medical Informatics Association* 27, September 2020, 1401–1410. https://doi.org/10.1093/jamia/ocaa092.
5. Daniel Morgan, Sanket Dhruva, Eric Coon, Scott Wright, and Deborah Korenstein, "2019 Update on Medical Overuse: A Review, *JAMA Internal Medicine* 179, 1568–1574, https://doi.org/10.1001/jamainternmed.2019.3842.
6. Harlan M. Krumholz, Joan Amatruda, Grace L. Smith, Jennifer Mattera, Sarah Roumanis, Martha Radford, Paula Crombie, and Viola Vaccarino, "Randomized Trial of an Education and Support Intervention to Prevent

Readmission of Patients with Heart Failure," *Journal of the American College of Cardiology* 38, January 2, 2002, 83–89, https://doi.org/10.1016/S0735 -1097(01)01699-0.

7. Sarwat I. Chaudhry, Jennifer A. Mattera, Jeptha P. Curtis, John A. Spertus, Jeph Herrin, Zhenqiu Lin, Christopher O. Phillips, Beth V. Hodshon, Lawton S. Cooper, and Harlan M. Krumholz, "Telemonitoring in Patients with Heart Failure" *New England Journal of Medicine* 363, December 9, 2010, 2301–2309, https://doi.org/10.1056/NEJMoa1010029.

8. Stephen Agboola, Rob Havasy, Khinlei Myint-U, Joseph Kvedar, and Kamal Jethwani, "The Impact of Using Mobile-Enabled Devices on Patient Engagement in Remote Monitoring Programs," *Journal of Diabetes Science and Technology* 7, May 2013, 623–629, https://doi.org/10.1177 /193229681300700306.

9. Joseph Futoma, Mark Sendak, Blake Cameron, and Katherine Heller, "Scalable Joint Modeling of Longitudinal and Point Process Data for Disease Trajectory Prediction and Improving Management of Chronic Kidney Disease," *UAI Press*, June 2016, http://auai.org/uai2016/proceedings/papers /160.pdf.

10. Michael Georgiou, "Developing a Healthcare App in 2020: What Do Patients Really Want?" *Imaginovation*, January 23, 2020, https://www .imaginovation.net/blog/developing-a-mobile-health-app-what-patients -really-want/.

11. Charlene C Quinn 1 , Michelle D Shardell, Michael L Terrin, Erik A Barr, Shoshana H Ballew, Ann L Gruber-Baldini, "Cluster-randomized trial of a mobile phone personalized behavioral intervention for blood glucose control," Diabetes Care, September 2011,1934-1942. https://doi.org/10.2337 /dc11-0366.

12. Donna M Zulman, Emily P Wong, Cindie Slightam, Amy Gregory, Josephine C Jacobs, Rachel Kimerling, Daniel M Blonigen, John Peters, and Leonie Heyworth,"Making Connections: Nationwide Implementation of Video Telehealth Tablets to Address Access Barriers in Veterans," *JAMIA Open* 2, October 2019, 323–329, https://doi.org/10.1093/jamiaopen/ooz024.

13. "Notification of Enforcement Discretion for Telehealth Remote Communications During the Covid-19 Nationwide Public Health Emergency," HHS.Gov, March 30, 2020, https://www.hhs.gov/hipaa/for-professionals /special-topics/emergency-preparedness/notification-enforcement -discretion-telehealth/index.html.

CHAPTER 6

1. Robert S. Huckman, Michael E. Porter, Rachel Gordon, and Natalie Kindred, "Dartmouth-Hitchcock Medical Center: Spine Care," Harvard Business School Case 609-016, March 2009 (Revised September 2010), https://www.hbs.edu/faculty/Pages/item.aspx?num=37097.

2. Jurgen Unutzer, Wayne J Katon, Ming-Yu Fan, Michael C Schoenbaum, Elizabeth H B Lin, Richard D Della Penna, and Diane Powers, "Long-Term Cost Effects of Collaborative Care for Late-life Depression," *American Journal of Managed Care* 14, February 18, 2008, 95–100, PMID: 18269305.

3. Hoangmai H. Pham, Deborah Schrag, Ann S. O'Malley, Beny Wu, and Peter B. Bach, "Care Patterns in Medicare and Their Implications for Pay for Performance," *New England Journal of Medicine* 356, March 15, 2017, 1130–1139. https://doi.org/10.1056/NEJMsa063979.

4. Hannah L Semigran, Jeffrey A Linder, Courtney Gidengil, and Ateev Mehrotra, "Evaluation of Symptom Checkers for Self Diagnosis and Triage: Audit Study," *BMJ* 351, July 8, 2015, https://doi.org/10.1136/bmj.h3480.
5. Hannah L. Semigran, David M. Levine, Shantanu Nundy, and Ateev Mehrotra, "Comparison of Physician and Computer Diagnostic Accuracy," *JAMA Internal Medicine* 176, December 2016, 1860–1861, https://doi.org/10.1001/jamainternmed.2016.6001.
6. Michael L. Barnett, Dhruv Boddupalli, Shantanu Nundy, and David W. Bates, "Comparative Accuracy of Diagnosis by Collective Intelligence of Multiple Physicians vs Individual Physicians," *JAMA Network Open*, March 2019, https://doi.org/10.1001/jamanetworkopen.2019.0096.
7. Hannah Byrnes-Enoch, Jesse Singer, DO, MPH, and Dave A. Chokshi, "Improving Access to Specialist Expertise via eConsult in a Safety-Net Health System," *NEJM Catalyst*, April 6, 2017, https://catalyst.nejm.org/doi/full/10.1056/CAT.17.0500.

CHAPTER 7

1. Saul Weiner, Alan Schwartz, Frances Weaver, and Julie Goldberg, "Contextual Errors and Failures in Individualizing Patient Care: A Multicenter Study." *Annals of Internal Medicine* 153, July 20, 2010, 69–75. https://doi.org/10.7326/0003-4819-153-2-201007200-00002.
2. Alan Schwartz, Saul Weiner, Frances Weaver, Rachel Yudkowsky. Gunjan Sharma, Amy Binns-Calvey, Ben Preyss, and Neil Jordan, "Uncharted Territory: Measuring Costs of Diagnostic Errors Outside the Medical Record," *BMJ Quality & Safety* 12, November 2012, 918–924, https://dx.doi.org/10.1136/bmjqs-2012-000832.
3. Alexander Billioux, Katherine Verlander, Susan Anthony, and Dawn Alley, "Standardized Screening for Health-Related Social Needs in Clinical Settings," NAM.edu/Perspectives, May 30, 2017, 1–9, https://nam.edu/wp-content/uploads/2017/05/Standardized-Screening-for-Health-Related-Social-Needs-in-Clinical-Settings.pdf.
4. AHRQ: Digital Healthcare Research, "Integrating Contextual Factors into Clinical Decision Support to Reduce Contextual Error and Improve Outcomes in Ambulatory Care (Illinois)," accessed November 3, 2020, https://digital.ahrq.gov/ahrq-funded-projects/integrating-contextual-factors-clinical-decision-support-reduce-contextual.
5. Saul Weiner, Alan Schwartz, Lisa Altman, Sherry Ball, Brian Bartle, Amy Binns-Calvey, Carolyn Chan, Corinna Falck-Ytter, Meghana Frenchman, Brian Gee, Jeffrey L. Jackson, Neil Jordan, Benjamin Kass, Brendan Kelly, Nasia Safdar, Cecilia Scholcoff, Gunjan Sharma, Frances Weaver and Maria Wopat, "Evaluation of a Patient-Collected Audio Audit and Feedback Quality Improvement Program on Clinician Attention to Patient Life Context and Health Care Costs in the Veterans Affairs Health Care System," *JAMANetwork Open* 3, July 31, 2020, https://www.doi.org/10.1001/jamanetworkopen.2020.9644.
6. Arvin Garg, Mark Marino, Ami R. Vikani, and Barry S. Solomon, "Addressing Families' Unmet Social Needs Within Pediatric Primary Care: The Health Leads Model," *Clinical Pediatrics* 51, March 2012, 1191–1193, https://doi.org/10.1177/0009922812437930.
7. David R. Williams and Lisa Cooper, "Reducing Racial Inequities in Health: Using What We Already Know to Take Action," *International Journal of*

Environmental Research and Public Health 16, February 19, 2019, 606: https://doi.org/10.3390/ijerph16040606.

8. "Social Prescribing Linked Me to Art Which Saved My Life," *NHS England*, accessed November 3, 2020, https://www.england.nhs.uk/personalisedcare /evidence-and-case-studies/social-prescribing-linked-me-to-art-which -saved-my-life/.

9. Alan Schwartz, Saul Weiner, Amy Binns-Calvey, and Frances Weaver, "Providers Contextualize Care More Often When They Discover Patient Context by Asking; Meta-Analysis of Three Primary Data Sets," *BMJ Quality & Safety* 25, June 2016, 159–163, https://doi.org/10.1136/bmjqs-2015 -004283.

CHAPTER 8

1. International Association of Scientific, Technical and Medical Publishers, *The STM Report, Fifth Edition* (The Hague, The Netherlands, 2018), accessed October 17, 2020, https://www.stm-assoc.org/2018_10_04_STM _Report_2018.pdf.

2. "Teva Pharmaceuticals USA Issues Voluntary Nationwide Recall of all Amlodipine/Valsartan Combination Tablets and Amlodipine/Valsartan/ Hydrochlorothiazide Combination Tablets That Are Within Expiry," *U.S. Food and Drug Administration*, November 27, 2018, https://www.fda.gov /safety/recalls-market-withdrawals-safety-alerts/teva-pharmaceuticals-usa -issues-voluntary-nationwide-recall-all-amlodipinevalsartan-combination.

3. Zoë Slote Morris, Steven Wooding, and Jonathan Grant, "The Answer Is 17 Years, What Is the Question: Understanding Time Lags in Translational Research," *Journal of the Royal Society of Medicine* 104, December 2011, 510–520, https://dx.doi.org/10.1258/jrsm.2011.110180.

4. Aliza K. Fink, Deena R. Loeffler, Bruce C. Marshall, Christopher H. Gross, and Wayne J. Morgan, "Data That Empower: The Success and Promise of CF Patient Registries," *Pediatric Pulmonology* 52, November 2017, S44– S51, https://doi.org/10.1002/ppul.23790.

5. Cystic Fibrosis Foundation, *2018 Patient Registry Annual Data Report*, Bethesda, MD, 2019, accessed October 17, 2020, https://www.cff.org /Research/Researcher-Resources/Patient-Registry/2018-Patient-Registry -Annual-Data-Report.pdf.

6. Sanjeev Arora, Karla Thornton, Glen Murata, Paulina Deming, Summers Kalishman, Denise Dion, Brooke Parish, Thomas Burke, Wesley Pak, Jeffrey Dunkelberg, Martin Kistin, M.D., John Brown, Steven Jenkusky, Miriam Komaromy, and Clifford Qualls, "Outcomes of Treatment for Hepatitis C Virus Infection by Primary Care Providers," *New England Journal of Medicine* 364, June 1, 2011, 2199–2207, https://doi.org/10.1056 /NEJMoa1009370.

7. Aravind Krishnan, Tim Xu, Susan Hutfless, Angela Park, Thomas Stasko, Allison T. Vidimos, Barry Leshin, Brett M. Coldiron, Richard G. Bennett, Victor J. Marks, Rebecca Brandt, Martin A. Makary, John G. Albertini, and the American College of Mohs Surgery Improving Wisely Study Group, "Outlier Practice Patterns in Mohs Micrographic Surgery: Defining the Problem and a Proposed Solution," *JAMA Dermatology* 153, June 1, 2017, 565–570, https://doi.org/10.1001/jamadermatol.2017.1450.

8. John G. Albertini, Peiqi Wang, Christine Fahim, Susan Hutfless, Thomas Stasko, Allison T. Vidimos, Barry Leshin, Elizabeth M. Billingsley, Brett M. Coldiron, Richard G. Bennett, Victor J. Marks, Angela Park, Heidi N.

Overton, William E. Bruhn, Tim Xu, Aravind Krishnan, and Martin A. Makary, "Evaluation of a Peer-to-Peer Data Transparency Intervention for Mohs Micrographic Surgery Overuse," *JAMA Dermatology* 155, August 2019, 906–913, https://doi.org/10.1001/jamadermatol.2019.1259.

PART 3
1. Cyclone Idai and Kenneth," *UNICEF*, accessed November 4, 2020, https://www.unicef.org/mozambique/en/cyclone-idai-and-kenneth.
2. Mozambique's health system," World Health Organization, 2020, accessed November 4, 2020, https://www.who.int/countries/moz/areas/health _system/en/index1.html.
3. Paula Span, "With Red Tape Lifted, Dr. Zoom Will See You Now," *New York Times*, May 8, 2020, https://www.nytimes.com/2020/05/08/health /coronavirus-telemedicine-seniors.html.

CHAPTER 9
1. Gordon D Schiff, "A Piece of My Mind. Crossing Boundaries—Violation or Obligation?" *JAMA* 310, September 25, 2013, 1233–1234, https://doi.org /10.1001/jama.2013.276133.
2. Zach Winn, "A Mobile Tool for Global Change," *MIT News*, March 8, 2020, http://news.mit.edu/2020/dimagi-commcare-health-0309.
3. M. H. Ouyagodé, A. J. Mainor, E. Meara, J. P. W. Bynum, and C. H. Colla, "Association Between Care Management and Outcomes Among Patients with Complex Needs in Medicare Accountable Care Organizations," *JAMA Network Open* 2, 2019, https://doi.org/10.1001/jamanetworkopen.2019 .6939.
4. Zina Moukheiber, "Concierge Medicine for the Poorest," *Forbes*, February 23, 2012, https://www.forbes.com/sites/zinamoukheiber/2012/02/23 /concierge-medicine-for-the-poorest/#5c62b1367624.
5. Sarah Shemkus, "Iora Health's Promise: Patients Come First," *Boston Globe*, May 3, 2015, https://www.bostonglobe.com/business/2015/05/03/iora -health-pioneers-new-primary-care-model/kc7V4W5V8OJ0gxFqY4zBrK /story.html.
6. John George, "ChenMed & Humana Sign Medicare Advantage Provider Deal for Philadelphia Health Centers," *Philadelphia Business Journal*, November 15, 2018, https://www.bizjournals.com/philadelphia/news/2018 /11/15/humana-medicare-advantage-hmo-dedicated-senior.html.

CHAPTER 10
1. Shantanu Nundy, Mosmi Surati, Ifeoma Nwadei, Gaurav Singal, and Monica E. Peek, "A Web-Based Patient Tool for Preventive Health: Preliminary Report," *Journal of Primary Care & Community Health* 3, October 2012, 289–294, https://dx.doi.org/10.1177/2150131911436011.
2. Centers for Disease Control and Prevention, *National Diabetes Statistics Report, 2020*, accessed November 3, 2020, https://www.cdc.gov/diabetes /library/features/diabetes-stat-report.html.
3. David A. Asch, Sean Nicholson, and Marc L. Berger, "Toward Facilitated Self-Service in Health Care," *New England Journal of Medicine* 180, May 16, 2019, 1891–1893, https://doi.org/10.1056/NEJMp1817104.
4. Kate Lorig, David Sobel, Anita Stewart, Byron William Brown Jr., Albert Bandura, Philip Ritter, Virginia Gonzalez, Diana Laurent, and Halsted Holman, "Evidence Suggesting That a Chronic Disease Self-Management

Program Can Improve Health Status While Reducing Hospitalization: A Randomized Trial," *Medical Care* 37, January 1999, 5–14, https://www.jstor.org/stable/3767202.

5. Kate R. Lorig, Philip Ritter, Anita Stewart, David Sobel, Byron William Brown Jr., Albert Bandura, Virginia Gonzalez, Diana Laurent, and Halsted Holman.,"Chronic Disease Self-Management Program: 2-Year Health Status and Health Care Utilization Outcomes," *Medical Care* 39, November 2001, 1217–1223, https://doi.org/10.1097/00005650-200111000-00008.

6. John Wilbanks, "AHRQ at 20: The Past, Present, & Future of Better Care at Better Value," *Congressional Briefing*, May 17, 2019, https://www.youtube.com/watch?v=awPIook3b6k&feature=youtu.be.

7. David Balderson and Kaveh Safav, "How Patient Navigation Can Cut Costs and Save Lives," *Harvard Business Review*, May 19, 2013, https://hbr.org/2013/03/how-patient-navigation-brings?autocomplete=true.

8. Harold P. Freeman and Rian Rodriguez, "History and Principles of Patient Navigation," *Cancer* 117, August, 2011, 3539–3542, https://doi.org/10.1002/cncr.26262.

9. L. A. Cooper, D. L. Roter, R. L. Johnson, D. E. Ford, D. M. Steinwachs, and N. R. Powe, "Patient-Centered Communication, Ratings of Care, and Concordance of Patient and Physician Race," *Annals of Internal Medicine* 139(11), December 2, 2003, 907–15, https://doi.org/10.7326/0003-4819-139-11-200312020-00009.

10. "UNICEF's U-Report: Using Mobile Technology for Youth Participation in Policymaking," *Centre for Public Impact*, March 22, 2016, https://www.centreforpublicimpact.org/case-study/unicef-ureport/.

11. Lawrence Casalino, Daniel Dunham, Marshall H. Chin, Rebecca Bielang, Emily O. Kistner, Theodore G. Karrison, Michael K. Ong, Urmimala Sarkar, Margaret A. McLaughlin, and David O. Meltzer, MD, "Frequency of Failure to Inform Patients of Clinically Significant Outpatient Test Results," *Archives of Internal Medicine* 169, June 22, 2009, 1123–1129, https:doi.org/10.1001/archinternmed.2009.130.

CONCLUSION

1. "Global Disease Detection Timeline," *CDC*, January 3, 2020, https://www.cdc.gov/globalhealth/infographics/global-health-security/global-disease-detection-timeline.html.

2. Adam Satariano, "Coronavirus Doctors Battle Another Scourge: Misinformation," *New York Times*, August 17, 2020, https://www.nytimes.com/2020/08/17/technology/coronavirus-disinformation-doctors.html.

3. Megan Brenan, "Nurses Again Outpace Other Professions for Honesty, Ethics," December 20, 2018, https://news.gallup.com/poll/245597/nurses-again-outpace-professions-honesty-ethics.aspx.

4. William H. Shrank, Teresa L. Rogstad, and Natasha Parekh, "Waste in the US Health Care System Estimated Costs and Potential for Savings," *JAMA* 322, October 7, 2019, 5101–1509, https://doi.org/10.1001/jama.2019.13978.

5. Frank James, "Warren Buffet: Health Care Bill Needs Redo Focused on Costs," *NPR*, March 10, 2010, https://www.npr.org/sections/thetwo-way/2010/03/warren_buffet_health_care_bill.html.

6. Kevin D. Frick, Lynda Burton, Rebecca Clark, Scott Mader, W. Bruce Naughton, Jeffrey B. Burl, William Greenough, Donald M. Steinwachs, and Bruce Leff, "Substitutive Hospital at Home for Older Persons: Effects

on Costs," *American Journal of Managed Care* 15, January 1, 2009, 49–56, https://www.ajmc.com/view/jan09-3891p49-56.

7. Shantanu Nundy, Jonathan Dick, Chia-Hung Chou, Robert S. Nocon, Marshall Chin, and Monica Peek, "Mobile Phone Diabetes Project Led to Improved Glycemic Control and Net Savings for Chicago Plan Participants," *Health Affairs* 33, February 2014: 256–272. https://doi.org/10.1377/hlthaff.2013.0589.

8. Marco Vitoria, Reuben Granich, Charles F. Gilks, Christian Gunneberg, Mehran Hosseini, Wilson Were, Mario Raviglione, and Kevin M. De Cock, "The Global Fight Against HIV/AIDS, Tuberculosis, and Malaria: Current Status and Future Perspectives," *American Journal of Clinical Pathology* 131, June 2009, 844–848, https://doi.org/10.1309/AJCP5XHDB1PNAEYT.

9. Partners in Health, accessed October 26, 2020, https://www.pih.org/.

10. *The Demographic Profile of African Countries* (Addis Ababa, Ethiopia: United Nations Economic Commission for Africa, 2015), accessed October 27, 2020, https://www.uneca.org/archive/publications/demographic-profi%1Fle-african-countries.

11. National Health Mission, "About Accredited Social Health Activist (ASHA)," accessed October 27, 2020, https://nhm.gov.in/index1.php?lang=1&level=1&sublinkid=150&lid=226.

12. Babylon Health, *Partnerships: Governments and NGOs*, accessed October 27, 2020, https://www.babylonhealth.com/us/partnerships/governments-and-ngos.

13. MomConnect South Africa, *MomConnect*, accessed January 15, 2021, https://www.praekelt.org/momconnect.

INDEX

ABOUT THE AUTHOR

Shantanu Nundy, MD, is a primary care physician, technologist, and business leader and chief medical officer at Accolade (NASDAQ: ACCD), which delivers personalized navigation and population health services to millions of working Americans and families. In addition, he practices primary care in the greater Washington, DC, area and is a professorial lecturer in health policy at the George Washington University Milken Institute of Public Health.

Dr. Nundy was a senior health specialist at the World Bank Group in its Health, Nutrition, and Population Global Practice, where he advised low- and middle-income countries across Africa, Asia, and South America on health system innovation and digital health. Previously, he was director of the Human Diagnosis Project, a healthcare AI startup backed by Y Combinator, Andreessen Horowitz, and Union Square Ventures, which he successfully built into the world's largest open medical project across 80 countries. Prior to that, he was managing director for Clinical Innovation at Evolent Health (NYSE: EVH), a population health and value-based care company, where he supported the launch of provider-sponsored health plans and accountable care organizations nationally. He is also coinventor of SMS-DMCare, an automated text-messaging software for individuals with diabetes, one of the first mobile health interventions to demonstrate improved health and lower costs and to be adopted by the World Health Organization's eHealth Compendium.

Nundy's work has been recognized by the MacArthur Foundation and featured in *The Atlantic, Rolling Stone, USA Today,* the *Wall Street Journal,* and *Wired.* He has been an adviser and speaker on digital health and artificial intelligence to the National Academy of Medicine, the FDA, the American Medical Association, and numerous healthcare startups and investors.

Nundy is a graduate of MIT (BS), Johns Hopkins (MD), and the University of Chicago (MBA).

For more information, please visit ShantanuNundy.com.